D1366591

Merle Robillard

ABOUT THE AUTHOR

John Seagrave grew up in the immigrant neighbourhood of Cabbagetown, Toronto. To escape the inevitable factory work, he signed up with the Hudson's Bay Company. Trained as a fur trader, Seagrave was sent up North to live among Natives and Inuit, where he learned the ways of the people and discovered his cultural identity. Seagrave was a "Hudson's Bay Boy" for twenty years before moving to Yellowknife and turning to a career in writing. He has published several short stories, including his "Caribou Stew for the Yellowknife Soul" series and one for *Chicken Soup for the Canadian Soul*. He also co-wrote the successful play *The Hudson's Bay Boy* with playwright/director Ben Nind. The play toured nationally, to rave reviews.

Seagrave lives in Yellowknife with his wife, Lisa, and newborn daughter, Anna. He continues to be a storyteller and dreams of touching as many hearts as he can with his stories.

In praise of the play *The Hudson's Bay Boy* by John Seagrave, which debuted in Yellowknife in February 2003:

"The storyline is epic, the twirl of events punctuated with bouts of singing, carousing, and drinking; a freewheeling comic takeoff from historical events. Everything is turned around topsy-turvy; even the acronym for the Hudson's Bay Company (HBC) wheels in as a sprightly Gilbert and Sullivan satirical routine titled Here Before Christ ... Nothing remains sacred, high-strung maybe, lubricated by laughter and occasional bouts of sadness and even tragedy, but sacred, no."
—**Ned Bobkoff**, Reviewer, Scene 4, Toronto, ON

"It struts outside our current political climate in the way that children do; in the way that the north has allowed us to live. There is a wealth of sharing, joy, and innocence that is rarely seen in contemporary theatre. And it told the truth. I know this because I have been there."
—**Ina Murray**, Executive Director, Northern Arts and Cultural Centre, Yellowknife, NWT

"Watching *The Hudson's Bay Boy* is like a wild trip on a careening Ski-Doo."
—**Bob Blackhall**, Director, Ft. Langley Heritage Society, Ft. Langley, BC

"... As a long-time theatre-goer, actor, director, producer, and instructor, I can tell when I see something that's exceptional .... Now I've never been up north but I sure felt like I had a much better understanding of what it might be like after seeing the show. Thank you for enlightening me about our great country."
—**Larry Reese**, Red Deer College, Red Deer, AB

"*The Hudson's Bay Boy* is a high-energy, hilarious, and sometimes touching series of stories of John Seagrave's recent experience working for the Hudson's Bay ... Although it is essentially a comedy, the play does not shy from the unbalanced relations between the Hudson's Bay and its trappers ... It is a joy to watch."
—**Lee Maracle**, Vancouver, BC

John Seagrave's Hudson's Bay Company Postings
Ontario, Manitoba, Saskatchewan, Northwest Territories, Nunavut

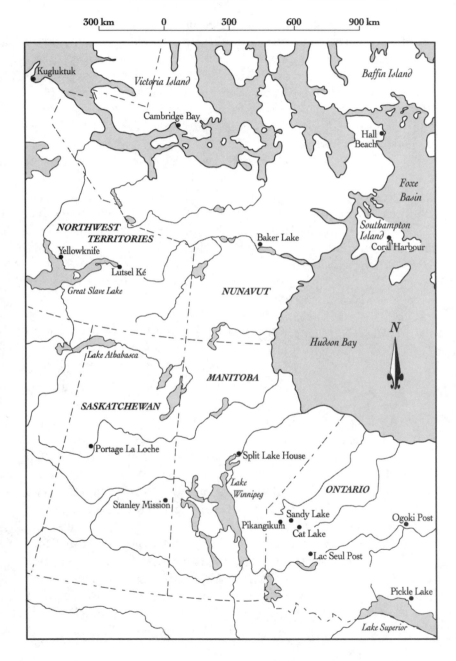

THE
HUDSON'S BAY BOY

From Cabbagetown to Rupert's Land

JOHN J. SEAGRAVE

FIFTH
HOUSE

Cover and interior design by Kathy Aldous-Schleindl
Edited by Meaghan Craven
Copyedited by Alex Frazer-Harrison
Proofread by Ann Sullivan
Scans by St. Solo Computer Graphics

The publisher gratefully acknowledges the support of The Canada Council for the Arts and the Department of Canadian Heritage.

 **Canada Council** **Conseil des Arts**
for the Arts **du Canada**

We acknowledge the financial support of the Government of Canada through the Book Publishing Industry Development Program for our publishing activities.

Printed in Canada by Friesens

04 05 06 07 08 / 5 4 3 2 1

First published in the United States in 2005 by
Fitzhenry & Whiteside
121 Harvard Avenue, Suite 2
Allston, MA 02134

National Library of Canada Cataloguing in Publication
Seagrave, John, 1959–
    The Hudson's Bay boy : from Cabbagetown to Rupert's Land / John Seagrave.
    ISBN 1-894856-44-9
    1. Seagrave, John 1959-. 2. Hudson's Bay Company—Biography. 3. Fur trade—Canada,
    Northern—History—20th century. 4. Canada, Northern—Description and travel. I. Title.
FC3963.1.S38A3 2004   971.9'03'092   C2004-902122-2

Fifth House Ltd.
A Fitzhenry & Whiteside Company
1511, 1800-4 St. SW
Calgary, Alberta T2S 2S5

1-800-387-9776
www.fitzhenry.ca

TABLE OF CONTENTS

FOREWORD

In February 2003, the Hudson's Bay Company was delighted to participate in bringing the stories of John Seagrave, a company employee from 1979 to 1994, to the Canadian stage through his autobiographical play, *The Hudson's Bay Boy*. Today I am equally delighted to be writing these words of introduction to *The Hudson's Bay Boy*, Seagrave's book of the same name. Whether on the stage or on the written page, his collection of reminiscences of a time gone by provides an insight into the lives of the thousands of fur traders who, for centuries before him, spent their lives working in Canada's founding business.

As a former "Bay Boy" myself, I have a particular interest in John's stories. Working in the north was a watershed experience for me. It was a simpler time—hospitality and friendship came naturally, without expectation of gain, because there was no notion of class or status. People were taken at face value. The lessons learned during those years of my life have stayed with me to this day.

Camaraderie, self-reliance, hard work, humour, tolerance: these are just a few of the characteristics of the Bay Boys. Whether hunkered down inside the walls of York Factory or in a modern house on the shores of Baker Lake, the fur traders— past and not-so-long-past—all had experiences that were remarkably the same. John Seagrave's memories are those of all of us who embarked on this most Canadian of experiences—a life of hard work, discovery, passion, and adventure among the people of Canada's north.

George Heller
President and CEO, Hudson's Bay Company

ACKNOWLEDGEMENTS

I always loved to read. My earliest memories are about reading to myself and to others, or being read to by someone else. It was difficult not to notice that most of those books had a page or two of acknowledgements. I never thought I would see the day when I too would be asked to sit and ponder a list of all the people I should thank. So at the risk of setting a bad example for all of the budding Canadian writers out there, here goes!

First, I thank my parents, Joseph and Cecelia, for emigrating from Ireland to this great land. I hope they see that, although they crossed an ocean to give me a better life, they only brought me halfway.

Pat Robertson, my Grade seven teacher, opened the world to me and taught me to question things always. I thank her for that and for a friendship that has endured for over thirty years.

I thank the Hudson's Bay Company for hiring me and letting me be part of something larger than myself. In particular, I would like to thank George Heller, Joan Murray, Debbie Keffer, Brenda Hobbs, Kelly McIssac, and Yannick. Two HBC retirees in particular have been very supportive—Wulf Tolboom and his lovely wife, Wanda, who is the original Arctic Bride. And thank you to Peter Brown for not firing me when my post burned down in Split Lake or for letting my goats poop on the front steps at Lac Seul Post.

Thanks to my brothers and sisters, Peter, June, Mary, and Richard. Thank you to Jody Wilson for being my typist in the early days—I still only type with two fingers. Thanks to the *Chicken Soup for the Canadian Soul* folks—Raymond Aaron, Janet

Mathews, and Darlene Montgomery—who inspired me and gave me the courage to write. And thank you to Farley Mowat and Pierre Berton, who led the way and put Canada and Canada's north on the map.

Thanks to Ben Nind and his family for believing in my stories before I did and for working with me to bring my stories to the stage in such a beautiful way. Ben also brought so many special people into my life that they are difficult to count— Michelle LeTourneau, Joel Benson, Sidd Bob, Keith Schooler, Murray Utas, Graham Cozzubbo, Dan Yashinsky, and so many others. And special thanks to two gifted healers, Heather Spence and Kathleen Matthews, who keep me going when my spirit is willing but my body weak

Thanks to my mentor Erik Watt, whom we lost very recently, and to his wife, Joy, who makes a mean roast of beef.

I convey my love and appreciation to Jennifer Johnson, who found me in the most unlikely of places.

A thanks and an important message to my sons, Josh and Luke—all fathers love their sons.

I embrace and thank the aboriginal peoples of Canada for sharing their lives and their land with me. You are the true keepers of the earth, and in time we will all look to you for guidance in understanding our planet, and you will teach us to hear her voice.

I honour the lives of all the Hudson's Bay Company men and women who toiled, lived, loved, and now rest on the far flung and arctic shores of this great land. They led the way.

In conclusion, I thank my lovely wife, Lisa, who is my family and brought so many of her family into my life. Marjorie and Brian Staples, my in-laws, I love you more than I can say. Thank you for making me feel I belong. And, Anna Cecelia Surusulitu, my baby girl, thank you for letting me be your daddy. I love you with all of me.

HERE'S A LONG NIGHT—AN ENDLESS NIGHT—BEFORE US,
AND NO TIME YET FOR SLEEP, NOT IN THIS HALL.
RECALL THE PAST DEEDS AND THE STRANGE ADVENTURES.
I COULD STAY UP UNTIL THE SACRED DAWN
AS LONG AS YOU MIGHT WISH TO TELL YOUR STORY.

Homer, The Odyssey, *translated by Robert Fitzgerald*

For my wife, Lisa, my true companion.
ECCE COR MEUM

INTRODUCTION

It was called "The Governor and Company of Adventurers of England Trading into Hudson's Bay." For the sake of brevity we now call it "The Company of Adventurers" or more simply "The Bay." When I was but a lad of ten, I was subjected to the same history curriculum as any other Canadian student. We were educated about Canada's aboriginal peoples, explorers, and the fur trade. We learned about explorers with exotic names such as "Radishes & Gooseberries," Samuel Hearn, Alexander Mackenzie, and Henry Hudson, all of whom mysteriously had the same names as Canadian bodies of water or other remote geographic features. Citizens of the United States trace their families back to the *Mayflower*. The Bay traces its origins in Canada to the *Nonsuch*, the Hudson's Bay company ship that started it all in September 1668.

In 1660 Prince Rupert and seventeen of his peers and drinking buddies convinced Charles II to grant them a charter, awarding them the rights to all trade from the lands that drain into Hudson Bay—this amounts to about two-thirds of Canada and a nice little chunk of the USA. Although the prince was a renowned military man, artist, scientist, and geographer, he never set foot in Canada. He was content to wait for the cheques to arrive in the mail. It was actually very clever of the Honourable Company, the HBC.

The Bay set up business trading out of York Factory in Hudson Bay and dispatched its first governor, Charles Bayley. This set-up proved to be valuable as the French and English were kicking the stuffing out of one another in and around the Great Lakes and Saint Lawrence River. War is bad for trade and the French had pretty well sewn up business in Lower Canada anyway. A group of French Canadian explorers and merchants eventually put together a company of their own, calling themselves "The Northwest Trading Company," also known as the "Nor' Westers." They were a completely different kettle of *poissons*.

The Hudson's Bay Company and the Northwest Company antagonized one another for many years. Business transgressions were usually resolved with pugilistic combats between underpaid and overworked clerks and servants of every description. Eventually cooler heads and diminishing bottom lines prevailed and the two companies merged into one under the Hudson's Bay Company's distinctly British-looking flag.

When the HBC boys once again had a monopoly in Canada, they spread across the Canadian landscape faster than you could say "McDonald's." When John A. Macdonald built the trans-Canada railway, the Bay had already surrendered most of its northern lands in 1860, in return for lands to sell to Mr. and Mrs. Canadian all along both sides of the transcontinental tracks. That made them the biggest real estate company on the planet.

In the 1900s the Bay began building huge department stores in every major city in the Dominion. The tiny outposts in the farthest flung corners of the country became less important, as did the fur trade. By the 1960s one could also find Bay stores in every medium-sized city in Canada.

At around this time, I was born. Two Irish immigrants stopped in downtown Toronto and started a brood. I was their second child, born in January 1959. Next thing I knew I was in Grade six, and my teacher began dropping Canada's history on me.

"The history of the Hudson's Bay Company is the history of Canada," she proclaimed. I believed her and she was right, to a certain extent. The Honourable Company was still out there and fresh history was still being made, although this was missed in most of our school textbooks. I was led to believe that the fur trade had vanished in the early part of the twentieth century. Imagine my surprise when I signed on with the company's Northern Stores Department in the late 1970s and found out that "north" did not mean the cottage country just north of Toronto that I had imagined. To the company, "north" meant Baffin Island, the Arctic coast, or one of the many places that do not appear on any map, *meta incognita.*

I was in my teens, as were most Hudson's Bay trainees, or "clerks" as we were called, when I joined the company. Many of the young men who joined ranks along with me came from Scotland, as had been the case for more than three hundred years. I quickly learned that the fur trade was still happening. Aboriginal peoples of every description still populated the remotest places, not just in Canada, but around the globe. My Grade six teacher had sold me a bill of goods! History was still being made and I was excited that I would be part of it.

Every old Bay man I ever worked with claimed that he had witnessed the end of the fur trade and the end of the north as it once was. Looking back through the company archives, it seemed every company man employed since 1901 claims to have seen the end of the fur trade, the north, and the aboriginal peoples of this country.

The core of my company service was during the 1980s. I witnessed the arrival of television to the Inuit people. On many reserves, where third-world conditions often prevailed, there was no phone service, and electricity and running water were just arriving. During my time in the north, airstrips popped up everywhere and Canada's aboriginal peoples were dragged, kicking and screaming for the most part, into the Global Village once described by the great Marshall McLuhan, another Toronto boy, just like me.

In 1987 the Bay sold its northern interests and concentrated on its retail interests through the Bay and Zellers. It hadn't much choice; Wal-Mart was kicking the innards out of Canadian retail institutions such as Eaton's, Woodward's, and Simpson's. It had to eat or be eaten. The Hudson's Bay Company, the oldest continuous commercial venture in the world, with more than three hundred years of history, severed its roots in the north in order to survive. The fur trade folded as prices at fur auctions all over the world collapsed.

I left the outpost communities when the trade ended and the trading posts changed hands. Years later, I found my memories hurting and resolved to record what I had witnessed during those years. I have few pictures because I found that I had to put down my camera to view the communities from within. I learned much from the various aboriginal peoples who took me in and guided me. I learned to love the people and the land, as they are one and the same. I continued to feel close to the company because it always made me feel that I was part of something larger and more enduring than my own life. In time, I became a respected storyteller in my northern home. Now I wish to share some of my stories with you.

Unfortunately, I must share these stories with you from out-side the communities that I learned to love so dearly. When I began writing these stories, I had already returned to the urban landscape where I had begun. To write, I had to close my eyes and search with my mind's eye for the people and the land that I loved—that I still love.

As the land and the people around me despaired in the changes that were occurring, I found I had to leave. You see, I loved them too much to watch them die.

JOHN SEAGRAVE'S HBC POSTINGS
—A TIMELINE

1979	Ogoki Post, Ontario
1980	Portage La Loche, Saskatchewan
	Baker Lake, Nunavut
	Sandy Lake, Ontario
	Pickle Lake, Ontario
1981	Lac Seul Post, Ontario
1982	Stanley Mission, Saskatchewan
1983	Split Lake, Manitoba
1984–85	Kugluktuk, Northwest Territories
1986	Sandy Lake, Ontario
	Cat Lake, Ontario
1987	Pikangikum, Ontario
1990	Cambridge Bay, Nunavut
1991	Coral Harbour, Nunavut
	Hall Beach, Nunavut
1992	Lutsel Ké, Northwest Territories
1994	Yellowknife, Northwest Territories

This curious young Inuit child jumped off a passing snowmobile and komatik to investigate this photographer. His parents had gone over the horizon before they realized he was no longer on board. They soon returned to pick him up. (Cambridge Bay, NWT, 1990)

STORYTELLER LOST

My parents met in a mushroom factory in Dublin in the early 1950s. They married, took a boat ride to Canada on the *Saxonia* (a trip they called their honeymoon), and settled in Toronto as they were unable to relocate to California. Five kids later, we had our own pew at St. Patrick's Church and were living in Cabbagetown in Toronto's inner city. We never met a relative while we were growing up because they were all still in Ireland and wondering if we were out of our minds living in igloos in Canada. Our friends told us my parents spoke funny and they could not understand a word they were saying. I would tell them my parents were Irish. They would ask what that meant and I would have to tell them I did not know. I thought it had something to do with having to go to church all the time. And eating lots of potatoes, while my friends were out playing, eating pizza, or sleeping in.

When I got out of high school, I took a job with the Hudson's Bay Company, which usually hired Scotsmen from the Orkneys but occasionally took on the odd Canadian lad such as myself. They shipped me to the Arctic to trade furs with the Inuit people. It was very cold and dark for six months of the year and I felt very alone, just as my parents must have felt coming to a new land. Most of the Inuit could speak basic English, which was good because their language sounded like Gaelic to me.

There were very few non-Native people there, but this was fine with me as I longed to spend time with the Inuit and learn their ways. They were a very likable lot because they seemed always to be smiling and knew how to laugh at themselves. Many generations lived together under the same roof. They also knew exactly who they were, which is what I wanted to know: who I was and why I felt like a cultural orphan.

One fine spring day during my time in the north, a group of old men knocked on my door and invited me on a hunting trip. They said we would be gone for three days hunting caribou, which I did not believe because we had no tent or other equipment. We travelled the whole of the first day and half of the night. When we finally stopped, it was only because a blizzard had blown in and we had to build an igloo before we froze to death. We sat in this igloo for two days waiting out the spring storm.

To entertain us, the old men took turns telling stories in English and Inuktitut. The adventures went on for hours—tales of danger, narrow escapes, great feats of survival and daring, and ancestors gone but never forgotten. When each of the men had told a story or two, all became quiet and everyone turned to me. It was my turn.

I told them of my parents' journey, leaving poverty behind in Ireland to find a new poverty in Canada. I told them of huge cities that they could not imagine. I told them of never knowing a relative or knowing who my people were. I talked for hours.

They looked at me and at one another in disbelief. One old man said it was wrong to let my people be forgotten because our ancestors live on only if they are remembered in our stories. A long discussion ensued in the Inuit language, after which the men broke into gales of laughter. I was hoping they were not laughing at me. I was also thinking it would be nice to have a hot plate of mashed potatoes at that moment.

I asked the old men to let me in on the joke. They told me that their grandparents had told them about when white men came in great ships and killed the whales to take the oil. The Irish whalers on the crew had taught them how to jig and had introduced them to stories of the green island from which they had come. It was said that the Irish whalers were great dancers and even greater storytellers. The Inuit called them *Sag-Li-Oonaat,* or "great liars."

The Inuit held storytellers in high regard. The men agreed that it was wonderful to have a young *Sag-Li-Oonaat* amongst them once again and asked that I take them hunting on the green island if I ever went there.

After that trip, I spent the next twenty years in Canada's north and now regale my own children and friends with stories of my adventures and the wonderful people I met.

The Inuit helped me find peace with who I was, where I came from, and why. I am a descendant of the *Sag-Li-Oonaat,* the people from the green island. As long as I can tell stories, all of the people I have ever met will live.

And that is who I am.

OGEMAH

It had been the best year of my life. In 1979, I signed on with the mighty Hudson's Bay Company, which still reigned in Canada's north after three hundred years. Being an adventurous soul, I had decided to flee the stifling poverty of Cabbagetown, Toronto's inner-city immigrant neighbourhood. Having graduated from high school in 1978, I was enjoying an exciting career working swing shift in a hockey puck factory in the West End. It was grimy, sweaty work, and I could not help worrying about the black, rubber-like compound that came out whenever I blew my nose. I was sure there was a better life out there somewhere. I had previously spent my summers as a park ranger in Algonquin Park and had cultivated a secret ambition to be a bush-guy and impress female tourists with my uniform and outdoorsy ways.

I do not know when the epiphany came, but at some point I suddenly became aware of the monotonous, soul-draining torment that factory workers face every day. It clearly explained the despair and premature aging I had seen in my parents. I had not understood until then the hopelessness of the path I had chosen.

Salvation came in the form of an employment ad I found in the *Toronto Star.* "Join the HBC, see the north," the ad cried out. It was illustrated with a very handsome young Native family, waving to a departing float plane, which seemed to me to be flying awfully close to the treetops. I applied to the Hudson's Bay Company with my puny resumé (without mention of my puck-making credentials), then kept the unceremoniously folded and crumpled ad in the breast pocket of my recycled, stinky, puck-makin' coveralls. The thought of being in that float plane kept me going through a very hot Toronto summer, during which I had seen more hockey pucks than Gordie Howe and blown more rubber out of my nose than I had on the tires of my little yellow Toyota.

In early November, not long after I had been promoted to the hot water bottle–making department, a letter from HBC headquarters in Winnipeg arrived. It contained a job offer, a hotel reservation, and a plane ticket to Winnipeg.

Three weeks later, I woke up in the Hotel Fort Garry, which was just across the street from Hudson's Bay House in downtown Winnipeg. I had thirty bucks in my pocket: twenty my sister "lent" me (at what I felt was an unnecessarily high rate of interest), and ten from the new hockey puck guy to whom I had sold my stinky overalls. The HBC office was practically deserted.

A rather pleasant fellow named Len greeted me with a firm handshake. He was from the Garden Hill Reserve in northern Manitoba. He showed me the ropes and gave me a ticket to board the *Polar Bear Express*, a train that hauled folks from Manitoba up to the James Bay region of northern Ontario and, I assume, back again.

I was told I would be trained to purchase fur from the Native trappers and to run the little general stores the Bay still had scattered about the north. My destination was a little reserve called Ogoki, which was on the Albany River, Ontario. The people of Ogoki were Cree, like Len. He told me that the word for my position in both Cree and Ojibway was *ogemasis*, which loosely translated meant "little manager." If I played my cards right I would make *ogemah*, or "manager," within a couple of years. Well, that was all I needed to hear! I was determined to make *ogemah* and no one and nothing was going to get in my way.

I spent the following year in the single-minded pursuit of *ogemahness*. The first year of my journey took me from northern Ontario to northern Saskatchewan and then onward to Baker Lake in the Northwest Territories.

I quickly discovered that my youthful appearance was going to be a formidable obstacle to achieving said *ogemahness*. I was what you might call a late bloomer. That's a polite way of saying that I continued to struggle with puberty well into my twenties. *Ogemah* criteria seemed to include a certain older-and-wiser appearance that I was not able to muster.

It was in Baker Lake that the call finally came. It was my new area manager, Peter, who announced my promotion to manager of my own outpost. The elation I felt was similar to that of a young hockey player who has finally been drafted into the NHL. I flew out to Winnipeg on the next DC3, which to my good fortune happened to be pointing south and reluctantly keeping the blue side up.

After a brief afternoon of training with the fur buyer at the head office at Hudson's Bay House, I once again found myself on the *Polar Bear Express* headed for Sioux Lookout, Ontario. From there I was transported ninety-six kilometres by boat to an isolated island outpost known as Lac Seul Post. I had hoped to arrive in the float plane that I had seen in the ad I had originally answered, but in the end there was no one watching anyway and I was too excited to care.

The outpost there had been in continuous operation for

more than a hundred years. The HBC had hauled in the best fur in the country from the trappers there. Mink, martin, beaver, lynx, wolf—you name it, it was trapped there. And there I was, the newest *ogemah*. I had indeed arrived; hockey pucks were but a distant memory. Eight kilometres across the lake was the Kejick Bay Reserve. Log houses, no water, no sewage, no power, no phones, and the best trappers in Canada.

The house was comfortable, well, nicer than the shacks in which the Natives were living. The post had a First World War vintage, thirty-two-volt generator and a single sideband radio, so I was way ahead of the neighbours, technologically speaking. At 5:30 AM each day, I powered up the old radio and allowed the vacuum tubes within to warm to the orange glow that meant it was ready. If the conditions were just right, I was able to contact the HBC posts at Webequie, Grassy Narrows, Landsdowne House, and Sioux Lookout, all in Ontario. On a really good day, I could reach the radio operator in Thunder Bay and actually make a radio phone call. Such radio calls were my only connection to the outside world that I had fled. At least the local folks had one another. It often took years for a post manager to gain acceptance in a community.

Although the people were kind and understanding as I learned their ways (and tried much too hard to fit in), no one actually called me *ogemah*. I had referred to myself as *ogemah* a few times, just to test the waters, and was greeted with looks of puzzlement and, on occasion, laughter.

The life of a fur trader may sound like a glamorous one, but the excitement was punctuated with long stretches of loneliness. As a result of living in such isolation, I found myself reading a lot more than I ever had. It was most enjoyable leafing through the plethora of Hudson's Bay Company legends, tales, and memoirs. I learned that in days gone by, the Hudson's Bay "factor" (or *ogemah*) often enjoyed a lofty position in Native communities.

Frequently, HBC factors were called upon to be counsellors, doctors, lawyers, clergy, police officers, or undertakers. When one was in a pinch, one would seek out the HBC manager for help or advice. A respected *ogemah* could enjoy the prestige accorded to a chief, elder, or medicine man. Unfortunately, that was the case long before I appeared on the scene.

It seemed that *ogemah*-type prestige was fading, as was the fur trade itself. I felt that I was living through the end of a significant era, to which there would be no return. History had slammed the book shut while no one was looking, and I began to despair when I realized what I had missed. All the same, I found I was enjoying getting to know the trappers: finding out who was Bear Clan, who was Wolf Clan, who was a good hunter and trapper and who was not. Slowly, almost imperceptibly, I had grown fond of the people of Lac Seul and they of me.

The end had come to a long, hot summer of fishing, hunting, and outings with my newly found mentors from Kejick Bay. I had learned much from the Cree, including how to read the weather and when to stay off the lake, which could be whipped into a maelstrom when the wind howled straight down the lake from the north. Frequently the weather isolated me on the island, as even the most experienced trappers would not brave the waters of Lac Seul when she was angry and calling for someone inexperienced to challenge her.

It was on such a day that I was surprised to see a small boat with four people in it picking its way through the unforgiving swells and breakers on the lake. They were coming toward the post, and I knew that something had to be very wrong before anyone would attempt a crossing. As the tiny craft approached, I could see it was a village elder, Philip, with his wife and his son Andy, who was one of my trappers. Andy's wife was wedged between them, trying to stay dry.

Andy and his wife, Sarah, were very young and had chosen to start a family at an early age, even by their community's standards. Sarah had just come home from Sioux Lookout the previous week with their tiny newborn girl, Mequin, who had been born several weeks early. Mequin meant "feather" in the local dialect.

As they crossed the lake, Sarah had her back turned toward

the wind and Mequin was nesting somewhere beneath a tangle of blankets and jackets. I got soaked dragging the boat up onto the beach as the breakers crashed over its transom.

The four sodden and grim-looking figures scrambled ashore and walked a few metres up from the shoreline to the lawn in front of the post. Andy turned to me without emotion and said, "Our baby is sick. Can you help?" Sarah had just disentangled Mequin and pressed her into my arms. All four then stepped back, looking into my eyes. In my arms lay a tiny baby, wet through to the skin, with blue lips, unable to breathe through her nose, which was sucking and bubbling with great effort.

"What do you want me to do?" I asked, my heart racing and the awareness creeping over me that there was no medical help available for this baby.

With the lake raging, there was no hope of a plane or boat getting in. Philip looked at his wife and then at me, "But you are the Bay manager; there must be something you can do ..." Philip's voice trailed off as he looked at the panic in my face.

The baby was now quite blue, and although I was trained in CPR, there was no getting any air into that baby's lungs. She obviously had pneumonia. All of her air passages were blocked with a thick, green, sticky substance, which I was unable to drain off. "I'll try the radio," I shouted as I passed Mequin back to Philip. I thought my heart would beat out of my chest as I sprinted to the post.

I knew we had a slim chance of making contact. The weather was bad, my batteries were almost exhausted, and it normally took at least twenty minutes for the ancient vacuum tubes in the radio to warm up. I turned the radio on and waited a few minutes. The vacuum tubes were still quite dim when I impatiently keyed the mic and broke in on the HBC's private single sideband channel. "CQ ... CQ ... CQ... This is Lac Seul Post CQ!" My cries met with silence so I repeated the distress call several more times. No answer. It was early in the day, and the other posts had not yet turned on their sets.

I quickly flipped the switch to SSB Number 2, the channel on which we occasionally reached the radio telephone operator in Thunder Bay. "Thunder Bay ... Thunder Bay CJY-631 ... this is Lac Seul ... Lac Seul, do you copy?" Again, my queries met dead air, and I did not get a second chance to hail Thunder Bay. I watched helplessly as the lights on the radio faded out. With no battery power, there was no calling for help.

I raced back down to the beach to find that Andy had built a small fire, and the tiny family was seated in a circle. Their faces were calm, their voices soft. "No radio." I almost choked on the words in a voice that sounded like someone else's. Philip quietly motioned to me to sit in the circle with his family.

Each of us took a turn holding Mequin, rocking her, her family saying a silent prayer, saying goodbye. As I held Mequin close to my face, I felt a soft warm breath on my cheek, almost a sigh, and then she was gone. It was the most beautiful and peaceful journey I had ever witnessed. Mequin's passing had a profound effect on me. All the parts of my soul that hurt me softened and were released. All the despair and darkness that I had pushed down deep inside of me, so long ago, moved away from me. All that had happened in my life before that moment became pure and clear and ceased to reside in the places that we all pretend we don't have inside us and rarely visit.

In that gentle moment, Mequin's gentle moment, my life was saved. Sitting in that small circle of love, warmed by the fire, under the cloudy sky, a small family and a tiny girl had created a circle of peace. And there was room for me in that circle. Philip and his wife sang several traditional songs, which I could feel but did not understand.

We all stood and walked back to the boat, which was now sitting still as the lake had calmed when we were not looking. Philip's family boarded the boat, and I leaned into the bow to help Philip push it off the beach. Philip leaped into the boat, turned to face me, and called out, "*Ogemah*, thank you." He turned away and the family took Mequin home. One last time.

I walked around the shoreline of the island until dark. Seeing it all for the first time, my heart bursting. I stopped and sat by the dying embers of Mequin's circle of fire and watched the sun dip behind Kejick Bay. I put my hand to my face, where Mequin had touched me with her last breath. I became breathless and closed my eyes. It was there I sat, waiting for the sun to return.

YOSEPH'S LUNCH BOX

I had finished high school, but I still didn't know what I wanted to be when I grew up. There was no doubt in my mind that I needed to move on to post-secondary education, despite the many obstacles that I found in my way.

My parents had emigrated from Ireland in the 1950s in search of the promised land and a better life. Their migration to Canada was undertaken for the benefit of their offspring as well as for themselves. Growing up in downtown Toronto, we didn't have much, but we were better off than many and surrounded by people just like us.

The neighbourhood was populated with newly arrived immigrants from just about everywhere. We were all the same because we were all different. Most of our parents worked in the many factories that were once the centre of Toronto's industrial core. My mom worked at the Neilson's Chocolate plant on Gladstone Avenue in the West End. She smelled pretty good when she came home each day, but she always looked tired. Her hands were the rough hands of a working woman whose day was only beginning when she came home to her five children. My dad had landed a job as an apprentice electrician for the E. L. Ruddy Company as soon as he stepped off the boat, and he kept it until the day he retired, for that was the way of things for the working man.

My elder sister planned and executed her education like a well-plotted military campaign. Her education did get off to a rough start, though, when her Grade one teacher at Ossington Elementary put her in "speech class" because she said "one, two, tree" rather than "one, two, three" like everyone else. Later realizing that "tree" was a "three" in our Irish household, she was paroled back to her regular class. She knocked off elementary school, high school, and then York University, just as she had planned. Hard work and student loans got her through the tough financial parts of the scheme. She became a special education teacher for the Catholic School Board, finding her niche on the first try. I, on the other hand, hit a wall after graduating from Bloor Collegiate.

I knew that I wanted to live in the north as I had spent all my summers working in Algonquin Park, about 270 kilometres northeast of Toronto. The thought of being a park ranger appealed to me although I was not prepared to survive four more years of formal education in order to get my own "Smokey the Bear" hat. I decided to take a year or two off to determine what I wanted to do with my life. And to earn enough money to get myself through school without going thousands of dollars into debt as my sister had.

I tried many jobs in an attempt to discover a situation where I could earn a decent wage but not lose my mind in the process. I worked at Neilson's, making chocolate bars to feed the hungry masses. Then I tried my hand at Alcan as a blast furnace "rake man" for an aluminum smelter; that lasted one day because my work boots melted. I tried working on an assembly line making hockey helmets at Winwell, but I found that too monotonous to bear. Then I lucked into a well-paying job at Viceroy, a rubber factory, where I was sent directly to the steam presses that cooked and cured hot water bottles. I caught on to the hot water bottle gig rather quickly. It was a stinky job because the plant always smelled of burned rubber. I had brought in my old portable tape deck so I could listen to my John Lennon tapes while I worked. My favourite tune was "Imagine." Ah, John Lennon, the "working-class hero."

The factory was powered by steam, giving the place the appearance of a cross between a medieval chamber of horrors and a Victorian-era sweatshop. The huge boilers, which generated the steam, lay beneath the shop floor; you could feel them vibrate when they were fired up. The antique power plant was oil-fired, but there remained evidence that the boilers had once been stoked with coal. There were windows on the place, even though no one had been able to see out of them since the Depression. The glass had been rendered permanently opaque by all the airborne chemicals, coal dust, and rubber particles, long before I was born.

Most of the personnel in the factory were the same age as my parents. They were immigrants as well, as I learned from conversations held in the rubber-encrusted coffee room. I chuckled to myself at the thought of how ironic it was that, despite my parents' migration that was intended to give me the opportunity to better myself, I had literally ended up in a rubber room.

The older men who worked in the plant were DPs, or displaced persons, who immigrated to Canada after the chaos of the Second World War. I found I enjoyed the company of the older fellows as they often spoke of how well their children had done in Canada. That was what immigration was all about: finding a better world in which to raise your family.

Of all the crusty old "rubbernecks," as they called themselves, I enjoyed the company of Yoseph the most. He was just weeks

This is the street where I lived most of my childhood. It is set in the centre of an industrial area. That is a slaughterhouse at the end of the street by the tracks. Across the street was the parking garage, or "barns," which housed the city's fleet of diesel buses. (Toronto, ON, 1978)

away from retirement and was looking forward to selling his house and living at his cottage in Muskoka, where his grand-children would gather to holiday each summer. I was impressed by the interesting old man who had come to Canada with noth-ing, bought a house and cottage, and put three children through university, all on a lifetime of factory worker's wages. Yoseph con-stantly showed me pictures of his grandchildren, usually at the cottage, and boasted of the achievements of his children. Yoseph's lunch box was so stuffed with photos of his family that I was sure he would starve to death on the rations he would be able to squeeze into the remaining space.

Yoseph treated me as he would any of his grandsons. He was kind, attentive, and showed me all the tricks of the trade that would save me a lot of work. He had a wonderful technique of making a grilled cheese sandwich, using the steam press in the hot water bottle department. Yoseph liked to show off how fit he was by inflating a hot water bottle with his lungs. I tried it myself and made him laugh as I made farting noises while trying to duplicate his feat. The old man was a good listener; I told him of my dreams of the north. He scolded me for not staying in school and offered to mould my genitals in a steam press if I didn't get back to school the next semester.

When the Friday of Yoseph's retirement arrived, I slipped a case of beer into the locker room so we could have a celebration after his last shift. There were twelve of us on the B shift and that meant that we would have only one beer each, but Yoseph didn't mind. What he did mind was that I had also brought my tape deck to his farewell soiree, and it was now belching out "Bat Out of Hell" at full volume. We tossed the warm beers down our rubbery throats and followed Yoseph to the punch clock, so he could punch out one last time.

Yoseph opened his lunch box and pocketed his precious family photos. He then passed the battered box to a young man who had been hired to work on the hot water bottle press, allowing me to graduate to making hockey pucks. I must have looked disappointed that I had not inherited the lunch box because Yoseph then waved a finger at me and said loudly enough for all to hear, "You don't need a lunch box; you don't need to be here. If I was your fodder, I'd kick your butt back into school and get rid of that awful music!"

With that, Yoseph punched out and stood beside the clock until he had shaken every rough and dirty hand that was pushed his way.

"Goodbye," I said, trying to look like a tough factory worker guy, even though I felt I wanted to cry. "Drop by and see us sometime." I choked on my own words.

"No," said Yoseph. "If you are here when I come to visit, I will throw you into the boiler!"

And then he was gone.

The following Monday afternoon, when I was on my third round of pucks, I noticed the shop foreman talking to a small group of the old-timers up in the office. The exchange looked pretty animated and ended abruptly when the group stormed angrily out of the office. The foreman came down the cast iron staircase and climbed up onto the platform on top of which I was cooking pucks.

"It's Yoseph," he stuttered. "He died in his sleep on Friday night; we just got the news from his family."

My tape deck suddenly seemed too loud. Everything had become quiet, as boilers and presses were all shut down at the same time. My favourite John Lennon tape had been playing, and the tune "Just Like Starting Over" had just begun. I had never been in the plant when there weren't steam blasts hissing all over the place or the clanking and sizzling of dropped rubber presses.

Yoseph hadn't been able to enjoy even a single day of his retirement. He had done so much for so many for so long, and now this. He could have easily been either one of my parents. I was stunned into silence.

The foreman shut the factory down for the night and most of the workers went home. I sat on a bench in the locker room, in the same place where Yoseph had sat every day for his entire working life. His rusty old locker was still empty, as there hadn't been enough time for anyone to claim it. I reached into my coveralls and took out the Hudson's Bay Company employment ad I had cut from the *Toronto Star* weeks ago. Holding onto this ad had carried me through the summer in the sweltering factory. I hadn't shown the ad to Yoseph for fear he would tear it up and lecture me, once again, about going back to school.

Sitting there in the darkened locker room, in the strangely silent rubber factory, I could not hold myself back from crying. This place had been Yoseph's whole life. I thought of a phrase from a John Lennon tune that I had always loved, "Life is what happens while we are busy making plans."

It was time to go north. I would set out to find my promised land and begin my odyssey. I could only hope that my parents would understand that although they had crossed an ocean so I might have a better life, they had only brought me halfway.

MY BROTHER'S KEEPER

We were all young men. Perhaps too young to be doing what we were doing where we were doing it. By the 1970s it was becoming more and more difficult for the Hudson's Bay Company to recruit people to live and work in Canada's north. High unemployment in the early 1980s had made sure the last batch of Scotsmen recruited were indeed the last batch. It was lonely work, but the brotherhood of the Company of Adventurers was a strong one, which to me defied explanation. I had made many friends within the company, but I didn't know what any of them looked like, as I had never met them in person. I had an accountant at head office, a bookkeeper, a fur honcho, several buyers, an area manager, and other assorted executives whom I wouldn't know if I had run them over with a Ski-Doo. Hudson's Bay House personnel existed as disembodied voices that were always at the other end of the phone, willing to support us in any way imaginable.

Seasonally, the company magazine, known as the *Moccasin Telegraph*, brought us up to date with all of the comings and going within the company. It also provided mug shots of Company personnel, which never matched their voices. More important, however, were the frequent communications I had with other managers in my region that put me on a first-name basis with more than one of my peers.

That was how I met Rick, who worked in the company grocery store in Churchill, Manitoba. When I was posted to Baker Lake, we spoke on a weekly basis. I ordered our weekly meat needs from his butcher shop. Always a card, always willing to help, Rick became the anchor to my support network out in the "civilized" world. Rick and I were hired on the same recruiting drive. He too was from Ontario, and we found we had a lot of common ground. He was a real go-getter, as I was, and was determined to run his own post sooner rather than later.

Rick was posted to Landsdowne House as manager just a few weeks after I had been appointed *ogemah* of Lac Seul post. I was looking forward to re-establishing our relationship, as we both knew we had taken on a big job for a couple of young guys from the city. In those first few days at Lac Seul, I attempted several times to raise Rick as I had thought his post was close enough to reach on the company's single sideband radio. I did not have a lot of luck, but I knew I would receive news of how Rick was doing from our area manager, who would be making a pass through our posts in the next few weeks.

Early Monday morning, about three weeks after I began my work as manager, an elder woman from Kejick Bay came to the post, bringing along her son to translate. She had received the news from a relative in Landsdowne House: the Bay manager there was dead. She had no other information.

I radioed Thunder Bay and made a radio telephone call to Hudson's Bay House in Winnipeg. My area manager came on the line and informed me that sometime on the weekend Rick had sat at the desk in his office, put the barrel of a .30–.30 rifle to his chest, and taken his own life.

I felt more alone at that moment than I had ever felt in my life. I'd lost my friend. And I had never even seen his face.

THE
COUREUR DE BOIS

When my parents grew up in Ireland during the Depression, refrigeration was a luxury, not a necessity, for people struggling to survive. Food had to be cooked thoroughly for fear of bacteria bringing "the sickness" into your home after a Sunday morning meal of eggs, rashers, and blood pudding. I certainly understood that people had to be cautious about such things, but there we were in downtown Toronto, many years later, the proud owners of our very own green refrigerator. One would think that in light of the technological developments immigration had brought upon us, it would no longer be necessary to incinerate every meal for fear of bringing "the sickness" in.

My mother was one of those "better safe than sorry" kind of moms who seemed to feel that there was no such thing as too much caution. So, she continued cooking in the typical Irish way, charring all meats, overcooking all vegetables (well, just long enough to remove any traces of flavour), and boiling the potatoes until they resembled cream of wheat. Meats were particularly difficult to identify at the table. Most meaty repasts appeared to have been cut from animals that were beat out of hell with a soot-bag, only to be thrown back into the scorching flames of the sulfurous and fiery hobs of hell on Earth, also known as the Irish kitchen.

A beef roast resembled a meteorite, while pork chops were able to disguise themselves as moon rocks brought to Earth by the latest Apollo mission. And, unfortunately, I learned that chicken meat cannot be separated from the bone once all traces of moisture have been removed prior to serving. Thank God we were Catholic and were not allowed to eat meat on Fridays. My brother and I would be dispatched to the neighbourhood chipper to bring home fish and chips for which my teeth and gums would be forever grateful.

Whenever my family went shopping, our first stop was at the condiment counter, where we would purchase several economy-sized bottles of HP sauce. HP sauce was created for Henry VIII, who was unable to tolerate the flavour of "high meat," a delicacy to the aristocracy of the time. He commissioned the royal chef to create a sauce that would be both palatable and cover all traces of flavour in that which he was eating. Later in life I would again be thankful to that unknown chef from ages gone by, when I found myself exploring the wonderful world of Inuit cuisine.

After serving up the grub, my mom would pass around the bottle of HP, which was so large that at the age of four years, I was still unable to lift it. The bottle would usually be empty by the next shopping day unless, for some reason, we had been unable to afford meat at every meal that particular week. The venerable "sauce of the gods" must have contained an impressive array of nutrients, as all of us grew up to be healthy and happy adults, despite the incineration of all known nutritional value within the other items on our plates.

To this day, when I think of my mother, I see her peeling many potatoes and putting them to boil on the gold-coloured stove that did not match our lovely green fridge. I realize my parents struggled to feed us on factory workers' wages, and I will always be grateful to them. But if I were to line up, end to end, all the potatoes consumed by my family while we were growing up, they would most certainly extend to a planet not in our solar system.

I waited many years before I was exposed to the exotic world of edible, nutritious, and uncharred cuisine. I discovered haute cuisine as a result of my employ with the Hudson's Bay Company. After arriving at Hudson's Bay House as the newest recruit of the mighty Company, I was treated to a two-day stay at the ancient, yet well-appointed Hotel Fort Garry. The Company paid for room service and all meals eaten at the hotel but not for drinks. As I walked to the hotel from Hudson's Bay House with my duffle bag and with my training manual tucked safely under my arm, I felt a sense of foreboding. Were they fattening me up for the kill? Was this the last meal of a doomed man? Or was it simply the Last Supper before I was (literally) thrown to the wolves?

After changing into my best blue jeans and T-shirt, I decided to dine in the Factors Club dining room at the hotel. I thought this would be appropriate, as I was soon to be a factor. I ordered the "steak medium rare," not because I knew what "medium rare" meant, but because "steak" was the only word on the menu that I could understand. My French Canadian waiter, who I fantasized was a descendent of the *coureurs du bois*, was patient with me as I fumbled through my order, in the end requesting a large bottle of HP sauce. Before I finished eating my roll and butter, which tasted like it had descended from heaven, the waiter reappeared with a bowl of soup with a lemon floating in it. I pointed out that I had not ordered the soup du jour and would never order a citrus soup anyway. I think I said something about lemon soup being as ridiculous as a beef milkshake. Without hesitation, the waiter apologized for bringing me what I later discovered was a finger bowl. I asked for another bun, which I found out was actually a "roll," and was told it would cost extra. I proudly pointed out that I was in the Factor Club, was becoming a factor, and had an expense account. Money was no object.

And then, *it* arrived. A sizzling pink thing surrounded by potatoes the size of grapes and what I surmised were green beans (I wasn't sure because I had never eaten them before). My dutiful servant then asked if I would like to have another roll; I accepted. I puzzled over the pink thing on my plate, which was obviously not what I had ordered. I sliced off a piece with such ease that I was sure whatever it was must be rotten. Feeling adventurous, I tasted the morsel prior to drowning it in HP sauce.

As the meaty gift from God melted on my tongue, I could swear I heard the Alleluia Chorus resounding from the kitchen. I cleaned my plate and before I could order another bun, there was my buddy, standing by with yet another roll with which I wiped my plate clean. As I signed for the meal, I thanked my wonderful "bringer of heavenly buns" and asked him if I could buy him a beer. He politely refused but thanked me for such a kind offer. I asked him what that was that he had served to me. "Other than the rolls?" he asked. "Steak medium rare, potatoes au gratin, and frenched green beans."

So that was a steak. I liked it. I decided to write my mother at the first opportunity and share my discovery of non-charcoal-encrusted cuisine. I laughed to myself as I walked up to my room. It had been the first meal in memory that I had not smothered with HP sauce. The adventure had already begun and I wasn't even in the bush yet.

FATHER
BOMBARDIER

An ancient de Havilland Beaver dropped me off in the middle of
nowhere. I couldn't even make out the airstrip on which we had
just landed. The pilot, who resembled Dave Keon of the Toronto
Maple Leafs, tossed the freight into the snow and took off without so much as a goodbye. There was no sign of a village anywhere, let alone the Hudson's Bay Company post to which I was
supposed to report. I was starting to think about building a fire
so I didn't freeze to death, when I heard the droning of an
engine. Finally, someone is coming to get me, I thought. This was
good news because I didn't have any matches.

A ferocious-looking Native man on a dilapidated snow machine whizzed right by me and snatched a case of eggs from the pile of freight.

"Hey," I yelled at him, "that's Hudson's Bay Company freight!"

He ignored me, as did the ten other Ski-Doo warriors who followed him. I was getting rather concerned that I would be held responsible for all the stolen freight. After one more pass by the motorized and thieving conga line, all the freight was gone, including my duffle bag. The sun was starting to set so I decided to follow the Ski-Doo tracks back to where they had come from. Ten minutes into my journey, a half-frozen, unshaven white guy pulled up on a spanking new snowmobile, with the price tag still on it. His ears and hands were frozen to a waxy white as he seemed to have flown out here in an awful hurry. He was looking around as if he expected to see someone other than me.

"One of my guys told me my area manager was waiting at the airstrip."

"No," I said. "There are no area managers here. I'm your new trainee."

"Get on then," he said. "Those bastards at head office didn't even tell me you were coming."

In a couple of minutes we arrived at Ogoki Post, which is on the Martin Falls Reserve, Ontario. I noticed the pilfered freight, and my bag, stacked by the front door. I was glad I had not mentioned the stolen freight as it was way too early in the game to look like an idiot.

I stepped inside the compact little store that was on the ground floor of the old mission house. Immediately, an unshaven Newfoundlander, sporting hip waders and a sweater that smelled of gasoline, offered me his stubby, black-nailed fingers for a limp handshake. His name was Glen. He was flicking at an obviously defunct lighter, attempting to light his loosely rolled roll-your-own. I backed away slowly as I half-expected to witness the resulting *poof* when the fumes from his sweater ignited.

"Grab a sleeping bag off the shelf," the manager, whose name

I now knew was Kevin, instructed. "Go upstairs and unpack your gear; Glen and I will put the freight away."

"Kevin?" I piped up. "I don't see any stairs."

The manager pointed to a homemade ladder in the hardware department. It was propped against the wall and led to the loft above by way of a hole in the ceiling, which seemed to have been hastily cut with a chainsaw.

I found my room in the loft. It was furnished with crates that had belonged to a staff member long gone. There was a dirty cot and a half-spent candle mounted on a sardine tin.

"Oh my God, what have I done?" I said aloud. I sought out the bathroom and found a recreational toilet with a stick shift on it and a sink that drained into a leaky plastic bucket. The bucket was full to capacity with grey water and untold quantities of sheared Newfoundlander whiskers.

"No soap," I observed aloud, then whispered, "*Yikes!*"

I had wanted to wash the gasoline Glen had deposited on me with his grimy mitt. I couldn't resist pulling down on the stick shift on the toilet and was surprised to look into the bowl at Kevin, seated below in the office. Kevin looked up and noticed me before I was able to shift into second gear and close the toilet bowl flap.

"Hey!" he yelled. "You have to put a kitchen catcher bag in there before you use it!"

I reopened the flap and yelled into the bowl, "Okay, got it!" It was then I turned and noticed an empty box of kitchen catchers and a significant pile of tied-up bags, each containing its own lumpy deposit.

"These two guys are way too fond of collecting their feces," I muttered. There was a pillow and blanket in the bathtub, which had no shower head or taps. I was later to discover that the tub was Glen's preferred place of rest. Glen had a room, but it was vacant with the exception of numerous sweaters strewn about, all the same, all smelling of gasoline. He had a rollaway cot just like mine and a sleeping bag that looked as if it had been used to wipe off the underbelly of a farm tractor.

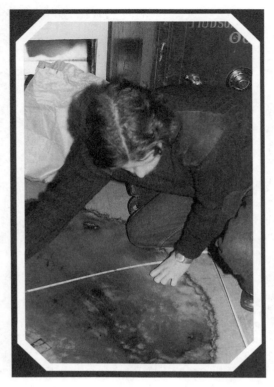

The Ogoki Post manager, Kevin MacDonald, measures and grades a blanket beaver brought in by a local trapper. Within a few weeks, I was grading fur myself and learning about species I had never heard of. The best furs were purchased late in the winter when the weather was the coldest. (Ogoki Post, ON, 1979)

More surprises waited in the kitchen: a table, three chairs, and numerous sardine tins, all of which were full of candle wax and cigarette butts. There was a sink, doubling as a large central ashtray, that drained through a pipe, probably into the leaky bucket on loan to the bathroom. There was a propane stove that actually worked, but from the looks of it, it only worked because my two roommates were in need of a cigarette lighter.

"No fridge. Jesus."

Kevin's room had a padlock on it, which piqued my curiosity. Being from downtown Toronto, I was able to pick the lock in seconds with a twist-tie from someone's kitchen catcher. Inside was a sparse room with an actual box spring and mattress on the floor, complete with bedding, night table, and lamp.

"What a bastard," I thought.

A local trapper discusses fur prices with the store manager. The store was unheated, so we had to dress warmly for work each day. The ladder leaning against the wall led to the loft, which served as the staff residence. We usually remembered to close the hatch when we were upstairs. (Ogoki Post, ON, 1979)

A scruffy-looking cat emerged from a pile of soiled clothing. Then I saw it. The fridge. It was lying on its back between the bed and the outside wall of the bedroom.

I snapped the lock in place just as Glen climbed to the top of the ladder and poked his unfortunate head through the chainsaw hole in the floor. He scowled at me.

"Kevin wants you downstairs; get to work!"

After disentangling myself from the quartet of leghold traps my pant leg had picked up on my way down the ladder, I reported for duty.

"Seagrave here, reporting for duty, Oh Factor, my Factor!"

"Don't be a smartass," Kevin scolded. "This is Father Ouimet."

"We live with a priest?" I asked.

"Who's this fresh-faced bostord?" the crusty soldier of God bellowed.

I reached out to shake Father's hand, which looked more like a foot to me. He declined my hospitality and gave me his duffle bag, which barely fit through the portal in the ceiling.

Father went to visit the local folks, and I engaged Kevin in conversation as I assisted him in taking the eggs out of the unplugged freezer in which Glen had displayed them. "Father Ouimet has been up here breaking trail to all of the communities as long as anyone can remember. He is a relative of the Bombardier family of Quebec; they give him the first new snow machine off the production line each year. We call him Father Bombardier but not to his face."

When we finished, the store was dark. There was no power in the store, and the sun had set while we were busy undoing Glen's best efforts. Arriving upstairs, I thought I would retire to my room and await the chow bell. I was famished as I had not eaten that day. As I lay on my cot, a "crunch" erupted from my sleeping bag. I inspected the bag in the dwindling light and was forced to press my sardine can candle into service. Below me was a grimy sleeping bag that looked an awful lot like Glen's. I inspected the bathtub and there was Glen, reclining in the tub on *my* new sleeping bag. I tossed Glen into the pile of used kitchen catchers and retrieved my bedding.

"Touch that bag again and I will strangle you with your own hip waders," I roared in his face.

Glen began to weep.

"But I am the senior clerk," he snivelled.

"Get stuffed," I growled while flinging his crusty sleeping bag into the tub.

For supper that night we had beef jerky and potato chips as my two companions were exhausted from a hard day of smoking and freezing innocent eggs.

Father arrived a while later and produced a deck of cards and a bottle of Bushmill's Irish Whisky. During the ensuing poker game, which bankrupted a drunk and weepy Glen, I had to ask

Kevin about the strange goings-on in this staff house.

"The locals don't like us very much. The young folks seem to like shooting at the building after dark."

"Little bostords," Father added.

Glen was in a drunken sleep by that time, clutching Father's arm and drooling on his cassock.

"That's why Glen sleeps in the tub. It's bulletproof."

"And the fridge?" I asked.

"How do you know about the fridge?" Kevin asked.

"Glen told me," I said, knowing Glen was in no condition to confirm or deny my claim.

"I sleep in the bedroom on the outside, where the Ski-Doo trail is. The fridge is also bulletproof.

"Little *bostords!*" Father slurred.

"What about me?" I yelled, jumping out of my seat.

"You're on your own, guy. Good night, I'm going to bed. By the way, you're sleeping in Father's room; you will have to get out of there until he leaves."

"You know Glen tried to poach my new sleeping bag," I said.

"I wouldn't be switching sleeping bags with Glen; he masturbates loudly for half the night. That bag should be pretty crunchy by now; he's been here for six months." And with that piece of startling news, Kevin stumbled away. He stopped briefly on his way to bed in order to fill a kitchen catcher.

Father and I played poker for another hour. I cleaned him out and hoped he wasn't playing with money from the poor box. That night, a crusty old priest, drunk as a lord and chain-smoking cheap cigars, taught me to swear in ways I did not know were possible. He tutored me in the fine art of cursing out a Frenchman while committing sacrilege against the Church in the same sentence. The whisky bottle empty, Father chomped down on his soggy stogie and headed for my bed.

"Goodnight, you little Irish bostord!" he chuckled as he left.

I heard Father fill the toilet in every conceivable way a toilet can be filled and spit his cigar into the mix for good measure. I heard him pull the stick shift and the contents of the bowl slop

37

down onto Kevin's desk in the office below. I was glad that I wasn't scheduled to train in the office the next day.

Suddenly there was an enormous crash, followed by Father yelling, "Bostords … *bostords!*"

Father had accidentally stepped through the hole in the floor that allowed us access to the store below. He was hanging by his elbows, a new cigar clenched in one fist and a small box of stick matches in the other. I struggled and managed to fish Father out of his predicament. Tossing him onto my cot, I took off his shoes and took away his smoldering stogie.

Day one, I thought to myself, not bad for a start. I used the toilet, flushed, and went to bed in the bathtub, as Glen had fallen asleep under the kitchen table.

NUNS,
MIRACLE FISH,
AND POKER CHIPS

Life as a Hudson's Bay Company snow gypsy was conducive to very short, but rather intense friendships. A century ago, when a Hudson's Bay factor could very well count on spending a lifetime in one location, lifetime friendships were not unusual. I spent much of my time with the Bay among the local folks as I was constantly picking their brains for traditional knowledge. When the local folks got familiar enough with me and forgot I was different, their oral histories would flow. That is the gift for which I am most grateful to my aboriginal friends and mentors.

Quite often I also found myself discovering unexpected friendships with the usually transient, non-indigenous wandering souls of the Arctic. First and foremost, the RCMP proved to be a fertile source of friendships, companionship, and that blast of testosterone a fellow finds he needs in his life from time to time. The members of the elite northern police force, or "Gravel Road Cops, GRC," as they were known on the bush road circuit, came from all over the country. Later in my northern journey, more and more aboriginal police entered the force and proved themselves to be fine officers and role models for the youth of their home communities. I recall meeting an Inuit RCMP member in a Chipeweyan community, of all places. We spent the better part of a summer renovating an aluminum boat I had salvaged from the town dump. We pounded rivets for weeks on that noble vessel, which came to be known as *Star Blanket*. The name came to us one sunny day as we lay beneath the upturned hull, replacing rivets. The sun shone through so many holes, it looked like a starry night under there.

Nurses proved to be more elusive, hard-earned, but very interesting friends to acquire. I suspect that the disdain many health care professionals felt for Hudson's Bay Company personnel, or "HBC Horny Boys Club" members, as they were known about the nursing station network, may have had something to do with the sexual habits of your basic "Bay Boy." Sexually transmitted diseases and unwanted teenage pregnancies usually ended up on the nursing station's doorstep. Frequently, a lonely Bay guy was found to be the root cause of the situation. It usually became apparent who on the payroll had done the dirty deed, when I would find a transfer request sitting on my desk on Monday morning. As a manager, I recall many nasty phone calls coming my way from the Nurse in Charge, requesting I rein in my lusty and youthful protegés.

Perhaps the most unlikely of all the friendships that came my way over the years originated with the local clergy. I obtained a huge portion of my "manly" knowledge from the many Oblate Fodders (Fathers) I encountered at Catholic missions all over the

An aerial view of Lutsel Ké, taken from an ultralight aircraft piloted by the local
RCMP officer. I only went up with him once and noticed him pull-starting the
engine with a rope. It was powered by a snowmobile engine, which I scarcely
trusted on the ground, let alone in the northern skies. (Lutsel Ké, NWT, 1992)

north. In Ogoki Post alone, a crusty old servant of God, Father
Ouimet, taught me to drink straight shots of whisky without
puking, play stud poker like a bandit, and swear like a longshore-
man with a case of the trots. A father in northern Manitoba
shared with me the formula for surviving a career with the
Honourable Company: never take a transfer to a community
with a name that has been prefixed with "Fort." He had surmised
that if there had been a fort required, as opposed to, let's say, a
"post" or "factory," the locals were most likely a dangerous lot.
An elderly brother in Lutsel Ké, NWT, taught me more than I will
ever need to know about gardening in the Arctic. And finally, a

female Pentecostal minister once tried to teach me yoga in Kugluktuk, Northwest Territories.

Of all the clergymen and women whom I encountered and befriended during the odyssey that was my career, no friends ever came as close to me as the nuns of the Sisters of Saint Joseph, whom I grew to love dearly. Keep in mind this is coming from a guy who hasn't set foot in a church for more than twenty-five years and who had a typical Irish Catholic "Smack in the Ear for God" childhood. The Sisters were a teaching order and were found hither and to in the north. The few remaining nuns of working age struggled to support the aging population of their order. Sister Maggie, one of the younger nuns who was the "best man" at my wedding, taught me how to play guitar and sing. I, in turn, taught her how to fish and play poker. We did not have access to poker chips and playing for cash was a sin, so we found ourselves playing for .22-calibre shells, which was not contrary to any known Catholic dogma. I hope Sister Maggie owned a gun; she cleaned me out.

Sister Maggie still tells a story that involves the only known miracle to have occurred in the community of Lutsel Ké and to have happened in my presence.

Sister Maggie and I fished together just about every day of the summer when we were both living in the community. The Snowdrift River flows past the back road near the airstrip. The fishing was unbelievable. The local Chipweyan people even referred to their land as "the Land of Fish and Chips." Bricker's Lodge, which sits right on the shore of the river, had made the grayling fishing there a legend amongst sportsmen. Sister Maggie and I, however, never caught a grayling there in all the time we had lived in Lutsel Ké.

Late that summer, a very excited Sister Maggie came flying out of the post office waving a letter from "Nun Central" in London, Ontario. The Reverend Mother, the order's equivalent of my area manager, was coming for an inspection visit. Sister Maggie was a fine teacher and was well respected in the community. I had no doubt the Reverend Mother would be pleased with the relationship Sister Maggie had with the community. Sister Maggie fretted about the visit anyway, but she was quickly put at ease by the casual manner in which her superior acted during her visit. In fact, all went so well with the visit that the Reverend Mother had a difficult time preparing to leave and wished to linger until the last possible moment. She was thrilled with the beauty of the landscape that surrounded her.

The Reverend Mother, after completing her visit, required a lift to the airport, which I was happy to provide. We arrived early, so she asked if we could visit the river, which was so close we could hear the rapids. Looking into the fast-moving water, the high-ranking nun lamented that the one thing she had hoped to return home with was some grayling. It was to be a gift for an elderly nun who had once frequented the north. I pointed out that I had a fishing rod in the truck, with a rusty old lure on it. I also mentioned that despite an entire summer of trying every angling trick known to mankind, I was still grayling-less.

Reverend Mother said a quiet blessing for my rusty old rig, which I then unenthusiastically tossed into the fast-flowing current. Instantaneously, I hooked and reeled in the largest grayling I had ever seen. I silently dressed and wrapped the divine pan fish and passed it to the joyous nun.

I felt like a fisherman who had been touched by the hand of God. As He watched over that generous and loving woman, something had guided my hand. To this day, I remain convinced that He touched the river on that beautiful summer day.

BLASTING THE RADIO

I carefully made my way down the ladder from the loft that my co-workers called the "staff house." Someone had come up with the great idea of sawing a hole in the ceiling of the Hudson's Bay Company store in Ogoki. The hole allowed us to access the staff house by climbing up a homemade ladder, which otherwise leaned against a wall in the hardware department. Personally, I would have preferred one of those shiny poles that firemen use to get downstairs, but the ladder looked as if it had been there for quite a while and I doubted anyone would be up for a change.

It was my first day officially on the job and I was ready to go. The sun wasn't up yet, and we didn't have electricity, so I taped a flashlight to my broom so I could tidy up a bit before the store

44

opened. Ogoki Post opened from sunrise until sunset, which was supposed to be an interim measure until we got a new generator. I was in Ogoki for three months and I do not recall ever seeing a generator there.

When it became light enough to find the front door, I unlocked it. I puttered around the store tidying up as I waited for my very first customer to arrive. Noticing that our display of rabbit snares was looking a little empty, I went about looking for reserve snares to stock the shelf. While kneeling on the floor untangling a coagulation of leghold traps, I sensed someone watching me. I quickly turned and noticed that an angry-looking old man, brandishing a shotgun, had entered the store unnoticed.

I couldn't believe that I was going to be robbed at gunpoint on my first day on the job for the HBC. If I had wanted this kind of thing in my life, I could have stayed in my old neighbourhood in Toronto. I had thought that I had escaped from this sort of thing. I raised my hands in the air as that was the only thing I could think of doing at the time. The old man eyeballed me and then reached into his packsack with his free hand. The armed robber pulled out a dangling handful of wires, plastic, and other unidentifiable electronic components. Just then, another customer walked in. I was saved! The new customer looked at both of us and nonchalantly proceeded to the cookie counter to buy some breakfast. The armed man started to converse with the other customer in what I took to be the local language. The younger man translated for the bandit. Meanwhile, my arms were starting to get tired from being held over my head for so long.

"Bill wants to know if you have another one of those." The young man gestured toward the tangle of wire in the old man's hand. "And he wants to know why you are holding your hands over your head."

It suddenly occurred to me that perhaps the old man wasn't robbing the place after all. Where I come from, if someone walks into a store with a gun, his intentions are quite clear. "What is it?" I asked.

"Bill says he was listening to a song he liked while he was out on his trapline. Then the radio faded out, so he shot it. You got another one?"

Trying to force my now numb arms to function properly, I sold the old man a new radio and batteries. He paid cash and left just as quietly as he had come.

This post was once on the other side of the Ogoki River. The HBC acquired this old church mission and converted it to a store. The loft was converted to living quarters. Out back, the graveyard spread across the area between the post and the river. We had to go to the river each day with a pail to haul water. (Ogoki Post, ON, 1979)

HARPOON MAN

After a full day flying east from Saskatchewan, I reached Baker Lake during a blizzard. When we arrived in the DC3, it was about forty degrees Celsius inside the cabin. I was shocked when I stepped out of the plane into the thirty-below temperature of my new home. A furious and blinding storm swirled around me. I couldn't comprehend how the pilot could have landed the plane when I couldn't even see my hand in front of my face. I watched each passenger in turn gasp as the arctic air entered their lungs. After finding our legs again, we all walked into the terminal, which wasn't much more than a shack.

I was greeted by Doug, who had been the manager of the HBC post at Baker Lake for the past few years. He explained that he was looking forward to a transfer in the new year to a more southerly community. Doug was a very pleasant fellow and he helped me carry my luggage to an ancient panel truck, which he then drove up a bumpy road to the community. I watched the town lights in the distance get closer and sat quietly wondering what I had gotten myself into. Doug was a quiet man and very earnest. He suggested that I should take a few days to get to know my way around before I reported for work.

I was surprised we could see the lights at all considering the blizzard we had just dropped through to land on the airstrip. Doug felt that we should get back to the staff house as quickly as possible. My new employer warned me to stay indoors, as a person could become lost three metres from his front door in this kind of weather.

I bundled up in my sleeping bag under several blankets and settled in for the night. I was tired from the long and perilous journey. I survived a restless night, which I spent listening to the wind howling outside my window and watching the curtains flap in the breeze. The ancient staff house bled cold air through every window and door. I shouldn't say I was completely surprised to find a snowdrift in the living room the next day.

I woke early the next morning and heard children playing outside. My curiosity aroused, I pulled my curtains aside and wiped the frost off my window. I noticed six little cherubs darting about in the snow, throwing sticks. I assumed they were playing seal hunter. Since I had a few days to get to know my way around, why not first get to know the children in the community? I watched the activity outside my window as I dressed. I donned multiple layers of long johns and was trying to prepare for the cold blast that I had felt the previous evening as I stepped off the plane.

Some of the children brandished broom handle harpoons while others had hockey sticks. The little Inuit hunters would strike a stance similar to the one a harpoon thrower on an old whaling ship would have taken. Then they flung their weapons with all their might into the nearest snowdrift. I found it all quite amusing, as the children were laughing, and I was delighted to see that they were practising their traditional harpooning skills. The game had most probably been taught to them by their elders and passed down for many generations. I was so proud of them practising out there in hopes of one day hunting seals themselves.

I decided that I couldn't possibly pass up the opportunity to get out there and start honing my harpooning skills as well. Looking around the staff house, I found an old broom that didn't have many bristles left. I snapped off the bottom portion of the corn broom and checked it for weight and balance.

I went outside and introduced myself to the Inuit children, none of whom spoke much English. I started running around like a mad fool, taking an Irish harpooner's stance and flinging my broom handle into the snow. Looking around, I was startled to see that the snowdrifts almost covered the staff house. On one side the drift blocked the kitchen window and almost reached the roof. I had never seen such a quantity of snowfall in one night. The wind had blown it up against every obstacle, creating a landscape of white.

The children were throwing little sticks into the drifts and running about like maniacs, having the time of their lives. After playing outside for about forty-five minutes, I was getting quite tired, although the kids looked as if they were just getting started. Suddenly, I noticed one child plunging his stick into the snow and then yelling loudly in Inuktitut. All of the other hunters came over. Several shovels were produced, and some furious digging ensued. I was puzzled, but then I heard a whimpering noise. I walked over to see what they were digging for.

They had just excavated a snowdrift to reveal a sleeping husky.

I realized that these children were not practising their harpooning skills! They were in fact looking for their dogs, which had been sleeping outside and were covered with snow during the storm. Feeling rather silly, I picked up my harpoon and sauntered home.

The morning after I arrived in Baker Lake, all was quiet due to an overnight storm. Children soon appeared with sticks and shovels to find their snowmobiles and family pets, which were buried under the drifting snow. Notice the rooftops had been blown clear of snow and the constant wind had blasted the paint from many of the buildings. (Baker Lake, NU, 1980)

ANOTHER MAN'S TREASURE

The Inuit of Hall Beach came from the communities of Baffin Island and from all over the eastern Arctic. It was a grouping of people from different parts of the Arctic and was typical of those communities that had sprung up around DEW (Distant Early Warning) Line sites in the 1950s.

The people clustered around the radar sites in tents, igloos, and makeshift shacks, seeking employment but also finding ready access to alcohol. Eventually alcohol and the loneliness the people (both southern and Inuit) felt being so far from their own communities led to frequent conflicts between the predominantly

male military personnel and the members of the Inuit community. The Canadian and American military at Hall Beach, in their
infinite wisdom, decided to create a village for the Inuit several
miles down the shoreline toward Igloolik.

Although the Inuit now found themselves at arm's length
from the military personnel, they continued to have contact with
them as they constantly rummaged through the dump on the
base. The Inuit did not waste resources and found many useful
materials in the military's trash.

It was inevitable that a chain-link fence would be erected and
an armed guard posted, as the military would not tolerate civilians having unrestricted access to their classified garbage. It must
have made sense to the commanding officer. Imagine the reper-
cussions if the Inuit were to assemble their very own nuclear
device and delivery system from the discards of the United States
military. They would most certainly become a superpower unto
themselves and would eventually become a threat to national
security. However, before the chain-link fence was erected, the
Hall Beach Inuit collected and transformed many interesting and
useful bits and pieces. A pair of kamiks was one ingenious dump
creation that sparked some controversy.

The women of Hall Beach were an eclectic bunch who
enthusiastically shared sewing and craft skills amongst themselves.
Kamiks and parkas made in Hall Beach were a synthesis of the
designs of the Inuit peoples of Baffin Island, Keewatin, and the
Fox Basin. The resulting clothes and footwear were unusual and
intricate—beautiful. One of the most avid seamstresses in the
community when I was there was Annie. She was one of the village elders and, though getting up there in years, was incredibly
spry. Although Annie's fingers and hands had been ravaged by
arthritis, she was still able to produce some of the most beautiful
clothing I have ever seen.

No one knew how old Annie was, as records were not kept
when she was a girl living in an igloo with her parents. If you
were to ask her when she was born, she would reply, "Just a
few days before freeze-up." Each day she would walk past my

window on her way to the village dump, where she would poke around with her cane in an attempt to find something useful. Some days she carried something back with her; on others she hobbled home empty-handed.

All Inuit wish to be useful to their families and to contribute their fair share to the collective well-being of the clan. In the past, elders who did not feel they were of any use to their families would leave the community for a "sleep death." A sleep death is a painless method of suicide by hypothermia and, in the Inuit culture, was once considered a reasonable action by someone who had become unproductive and a burden to the family.

At the dump one day, in her quest to be useful, Annie discovered a couple of dogs that had been shot by their owner. She produced a knife and proceeded to skin out both animals as she had been seeking some fur to make her son a new pair of kamiks.

I did not see Annie for several days. A week later, her son appeared sporting a very attractive pair of ornate, husky-fur boots. After showing off the new kamiks in the store, Annie's son went about his business as the water truck driver for the community. While delivering water on the east end of the village one morning, he was accosted by an irate woman who claimed he was wearing *her* dogs on *his* feet. The woman's husband was summoned to confirm the identities of the canine footwear, which he did. The dispute escalated.

Faster than you could say "mush," all the parties concerned (and many who should not have been), found themselves at the RCMP detachment, pleading their cases to a very confused, newly arrived corporal.

I'm willing to wager the corporal had not been trained in footwear conflict resolution at the RCMP training depot in Regina. Summoning an interpreter from the nearby nursing station, the officer started his investigation into the matter. The offended party, backed up by his entire extended family, explained that even though he had shot his dogs and left them at the dump, they were still *his* dogs, and he should therefore be given the kamiks.

Annie's son and his posse explained that the Inuit rule that applied here was "finders keepers." The kamiks were a gift from his mother, and they were *his* kamiks.

Word quickly spread around town that two of the largest families in Hall Beach were going at it again and that everyone was up at the RCMP detachment, raising hell. Annie grabbed her cane, sprinted across town, and headed directly for the centre of the fracas. Upon arrival, she yelled something that sounded pretty nasty in Inuktitut, while tearing the kamiks from the RCMP officer's hands.

Annie produced a nasty-looking ulu and commenced shredding the disputed footwear before the eyes of all of the concerned parties. When she was finished, the kamiks were unusable and unrecognizable. She turned and hobbled away with a very disgusted look on her face. The RCMP office quickly cleared of people and the incident was over as quickly as it had begun.

The RCMP officer realized that to police the community fairly, he would need an elder ally, such as Annie. There was no shortage of interpreters in Annie's family. The corporal and the old lady became fast friends; he consulted her on a daily basis to resolve domestic disputes of every description. Annie, in turn, was provided with transportation and was remunerated with sewing supplies.

The following week, I waved to Annie as she passed my window sitting in the co-pilot's seat of the RCMP vehicle. She was on her way to the dump with her new friend to find another treasure.

MEDIVAC

Most people who dwell in Canada's north will never admit it, but they really do live on the edge. There are no hospitals up there and very few doctors. All too frequently struggles for life and death are played out in the tiny nursing stations that can be found in even the most diminutive of communities. Although doctors and dentists do visit the remote villages occasionally, northern residents depend wholly on the nurses who staff the stations and outposts. Unlike their southern cousins, northern nurses take on a variety of roles. In addition to their work as conventional nurses, northern nurses are also midwives, health inspectors, pharmacists, psychiatrists, doctors, and bereavement counsellors. Frequently, nurses are also the only barbers in a community;

without them, we would all have resembled primitive *Homo sapiens* who draw water and hew wood. Their medical skills far surpass those of their urban counterparts, and the empathy and compassion they displayed to me and to others over the years defined humanity for me and became a measuring stick for my own actions.

They usually didn't like Bay Boys very much because Bay trainees had a penchant for fertilizing the neighbourhood and then transferring out of the community before embarrassing questions were asked. Even so, I have struck up friendships with arctic nurses that have lasted for years. I have sat through snowstorms that have lasted for days with them, hoping, somehow, that a plane would get in to pick up the sick and injured. I once supported a nurse while she helplessly watched the life drain from a premature baby who could not be saved as we were too far from a hospital.

The last resort in any medical situation is the medivac (medical evacuation). The procedure often involves placing a patient in the tiniest of aircraft, boat, or snowmobile, and sending them off, hoping there will be enough time for them to get to the appropriate facilities. Very often patients did not make it. Medivacs, successful and unsuccessful, are a fact of life in the north. You don't think about how precarious life really is in the Arctic and how far you are from help until one day you find yourself on the stretcher.

This is a story about a pair of friends who fell ill in the Arctic; about one who survived and one who did not.

I had been in Cambridge Bay, Northwest Territories, for several months, renovating the grocery department, when I met Sunita. We were attempting to squeeze a few more years out of the obsolete post. Cambridge Bay was one of the communities that had a reason for being where it was before the DEW Line was built in the late fifties. Cam Main, as it was called, was one of the largest military installations in the north, but the Inuit were there first. The area was known as Ikaluktutiak, or "good fishing place," and it sure was. The Inuit there had become commercial fishermen and had also built an innovative fish processing and packaging plant that was the envy of any outport in Newfoundland.

I found myself working long hours, late into the evenings, on most days in Cambridge Bay. It becomes tiresome seeing the same faces you work with twelve hours every day. One breath of fresh air each day was seeing Sunita shopping in the store. She always stopped for a chat and was pleasing to the eye and to the soul. She was to become a friend and one of those people whom you remember for all your days.

Sunita lived in a small staff house with her mother, who worked for the territorial government. Sunita and her mother stood out in the community because they were East Indian, of the Baha'i faith, and the only non-aboriginal persons in the village who were of colour. They were both beautiful women, but it was Sunita who turned heads with her huge smile, organic beauty, and sweet disposition. Many men from the community approached both women with love, or something like it, in their hearts. I even convinced Sunita to join me for brunch at the company staff house on one occasion. Although I was delighted when she accepted, I was equally deflated when she turned up with her mother as a chaperone. We had a wonderful time anyway and as we parted ways, I was pleased to have made two new friends.

Ikaluktutiak had been a lonely stop for me as the workload had prevented me from becoming involved in the community or doing any hunting or fishing with the elders. When word came in that I was to move on to Hall Beach in the eastern Arctic, I realized that I had no one to share the news with. It was at such times that I felt quite lonely and isolated in the north. Fur trading and working for the Honourable Company in far-flung outposts sounds romantic, and it was romantic at times. But that glamour was punctuated with long stretches of profound loneliness and, at times, despair. Transfer time was one of those unpalatable times in the northern adventure.

The night I found out I was moving on, Sunita made an unscheduled appearance at the staff house, sans chaperone. I broke the news to her that I was moving. We were both teary as she said that she was also leaving on a mission of her own. Her faith had called her to a vocation in the Siberian Arctic. We coincidentally had been scheduled to leave the community on the same flight. I was overjoyed for Sunita because she was carrying out a task that was dear to her soul. I felt I was as well.

After a long, silent, and uncomfortable flight together on NWT Air's Electra, we parted ways in Yellowknife. I had to fly east and Sunita had to overnight at the Baha'i house. We hugged warmly. It was the last time I saw her. Our lives had intersected for only a brief moment, but somehow they began to follow a similar course.

Hall Beach had two things in common with Cambridge Bay. It had a huge military site, Fox Main, and great fishing. I had to dig in, as there was much to do. That is always the case when a manager has the misfortune of arriving only days before barge time, when supplies come in for the year. It is difficult to make friends when one has to work twelve-hour days. I did not go out on a single hunting trip during my tenure in Hall Beach. I found the elders aloof, as was sometimes the case when the community had experienced a flurry of indifferent post managers over short periods of time.

After the barge was squared away, the area manager usually came around on a big inspection visit. This year, he was bringing his boss, the regional manager, around with him. Any post factor who was serious about his career dreaded this visit. I was no exception. I worked my heart out as usual, putting in twelve-hour days despite having just put in three twenty-four-hour days to land the yearly resupply from the barge. The morning of the big visit I did not feel well, but I put on my happy face and waited to hear the buzz of the company's aircraft over the community. I had asked my buddies at Air-Radio Weather Services to give me a call when they heard the company plane on the air. They didn't.

Shortly after 11 AM, the company party arrived. They did a whirlwind inspection and then heaped the appropriate amount of criticism on the store and warehouses, which "did not reflect the standards expected of an employee of the company." Visits would have been much more efficient if we had met the executives at the airstrip and had them pluck our still-beating hearts from our chests and dance on them right there.

The VIPs flew out and I wandered down to the warehouses to begin trimming the place to company standards. I found the diagram left behind by the lofty Bay Boys. I sat in the dim light and contemplated the reshuffling of about half a million kilos of freight. We were a little short-handed, as I had burned out the help when the barges were in. There are only so many Inuit willing to work for minimum wage. Having formulated the "one-man plan," I hoisted the first box over my shoulder. I collapsed to my knees as a sharp pain shot through my right side. I felt as if I was going to throw up, but I chalked the feeling up to the stress from the royal visit. I went home to lie down and called the store to let them know I wouldn't be back that day.

I had a visit from Sunita that night. At least I thought I did. We were fishing for Arctic char and discussing the meaning of life. I cannot remember a single conversation I had with her that did not start or end with the meaning of life, so this particular visit seemed very real to me. My mother also visited me that evening to chastise me for wasting my life working in a hockey puck factory and for consorting with "those" types of women. At about 3 AM, Richard Nixon was reminding me that he was "not a crook" when a young lady who worked for me dropped by to see if I would be opening the store the next morning or if I was still sick. She put her cool hand on my forehead and called the RCMP. The constables arrived to carry me down the numerous stairs as I serenaded them with burst after burst of unintelligible conversation. If I had been drunk, I am sure they would have laughed. However, I was delirious with fever and they were concerned for my life.

Later, at the nursing station, I awoke to the sensation of a rather large nurse's digit being inserted where it should not have been. After contacting a doctor in Iqaluit on Baffin Island by phone, the medical staff arrived at a consensus and ordered a medivac. I had acute appendicitis and they had to get me to a hospital in Montreal for immediate surgery or I was a dead man.

Three hours later, at 6 AM, my appendix burst. The aircraft was still three hours away. Richard Nixon was back and was now sporting caribou clothes and sealskin boots. I was wishing he would leave. Not because of his bad attitude, the blood on his hands from Vietnam, or because his scooped nose reminded me of Bob Hope. I wanted him to leave because I just didn't like the look of the guy, and what in hell was he doing in Hall Beach anyway? I figured it would be a good time to open my eyes so I did just that. Soaked in sweat and bundled onto a wire stretcher, I was on a plane lying on my left side. There was a nurse beside me, serious and concerned. She held me still as I was trying to roll over to get more comfortable, tangling the multiple IV tubes in my arm. I asked where I was. She told me that my appendix had burst. By all accounts, I was five hours from Montreal and three hours from Iqaluit. I remember thinking I was a dead man.

There was a fuel stop at Igloolik, 130 kilometres north of Hall Beach, where some genius rammed the landing gear with a front-end loader. A one-hour delay ensued for an aircraft safety inspection. I was definitely a dead man.

Suddenly we were back in the air. I looked to my right and saw a flock of snow buntings trying to keep up with the jet; they did.

Then, just as suddenly, I was in an ambulance, but not in Montreal. I was in Iqaluit. There was a doctor on board who smelled like peppermints. He explained that there was no time to take me to Montreal. "We have to operate or you won't make it." Before they covered my face with a smelly rubber mask and I passed out, I thought, am I ever a dead man.

But two days later, the peppermint doctor was hovering over me, saying, "You are lucky to be here. You should be a dead man."

And three days later, the area manager was there, saying, "You don't look too good. If we don't replace you, we will have a disaster on our hands."

I was in so much pain, I didn't care. "Okay," I said as I gave up my post.

"Do you have anywhere to stay?" he asked.

Twelve days later, I woke up in Toronto at my parents' place; that was way too surreal for me. I hadn't been home in years, and I hadn't left on the best of terms. I was much older now. I was a different person. My parents didn't know me anymore. Everyone and everything was right where I had left them. They were more confused than I was as I lay on their couch trying to heal. Conversation did not interest me. The dark clouds came for me and I descended into them. I would take short daily walks and then fitful sleep would overtake me.

I missed my post and the Inuit; I felt that I had failed them and myself in some way. Without the company I felt like a smaller person. They had made me a better man. Winter was coming and the trappers would be heading back out. I encouraged myself to get well and get back to send out my trappers.

In a month my strength returned. I visited all of the old places in Toronto to assure myself that they had been real. I listened for the silence of the north and could not find it. I looked at a night sky with no stars or dancing lights. The dark cloud lifted and released me. It was time to go home.

As the huge jet pointed to the east and rose into the gloaming, I rested my head on the window of the aircraft. An orange moon waited for us as we popped out of the clouds and stars began to appear. They had been there all along. I just hadn't been able to see them.

As I fell asleep, I recalled that when the Inuit have a near-death experience they are required to change their name. I fully understood that now, for the first time. The Inuit to this day tell me that I must change my name because the part of me that survived my ordeal will never be the same. I had been humbled by my own mortality. As profound as this experience had been for me, I had only done what the Inuit have done for centuries: I had survived. And I was going home. The company had assigned me to a new post.

Two years later, I had a stopover in Yellowknife en route to head office in Winnipeg. I ran into the jovial RCMP corporal who was once in charge of the Cambridge Bay detachment. We laughed heartily and got caught up over a beer at the airport restaurant. All too soon his flight was called. As he grabbed his briefcase to leave, I realized I had failed to ask him if he had heard anything about Sunita or her mother. He had. Sunita had arrived safely at her mission in a tiny Siberian village on the Arctic coast. One month later she was struck down by appendicitis. The community had no medical personnel, nursing station, or airstrip. She was with her fellow missionaries when her appendix burst. Sunita died that day.

Sunita had gone about her mission that fall. As I struggled to unload the resupply, she was struggling for her life. As young and as strong as she was, she gave up her life.

She left this world doing what she loved and, like myself, was aware of the risks she had chosen to endure. At her request, she was buried among the Arctic people she had come to live with. Perhaps she felt that she had failed the people in some way and wished to remain with her mission. I am sure her soul ascended to the colourful dancing lights of the starry Arctic sky to abide there.

Sunita, I cry for the parts of you that we missed and will never know. I cry for the parts of me that survived and I will never understand.

PRIZES, POTS, AND POSTAGE STAMPS

Baker Lake, Northwest Territories, is about as far as you can get from downtown Toronto, and not only if you are counting distance. An entire year had passed since I left Toronto and hired on with the Hudson's Bay Company. Based on a master plan to which I was not privy, the Gentlemen and Adventurers had seen fit to transfer me around the north like a snowflake in a whirlwind. It finally seemed as if all my hard work was about to bear some fruit. Despite being a snow gypsy, I had finally started to feel at home amongst the Thirteen Tribes that made up the Inuit community of Baker Lake. I felt that I was really beginning to

*These children are playing at the back row of houses where most of the "Pots,"
or Back River people, lived. The Back River people were the last and the poorest people to settle Baker Lake. They were mentioned by Farley Mowat when
he observed them in the 1940s. (Baker Lake, NU, 1980)*

understand their culture and social practices, but it wasn't until
my first Christmas there that I saw through those structures.

Back in the early days, before Baker Lake and before the
Crown actually knew how many "Eskimos" it owned, the Royal
Canadian Air Force set about tracking down and enumerating
the nomadic hunters of the Keewatin region. In the late 1940s,
the people were rounded up, which proved to be an exercise similar to that of herding cats. The Inuit were then organized into
communities so His Royal Highness could keep them warm. The
old folks told me that the Caribou Inuit had been minding their
own business at the time, wandering about in thirteen distinct

groups, following a social order of their own.

Before the air force created townships in Keewatin, there was some sort of caste system in place which I still do not completely understand, considering what a struggle it must have been just to stay alive in the frozen wasteland the people called Nunavut, "Our Land." I would not even attempt to pronounce the names with which the people supplied themselves, with the exception of the lowest caste. They were called "Pots" or "Back River" people. The Pots seemed to keep to themselves, were shunned by all, and were poorer than the poorest people I had seen in Toronto's Cabbagetown. Calling a person a Pot was a sarcastic way of saying, "You are so poor you don't even own a pot." The Pot caste was still visible a generation after the Crown brought "communities" to the north; the "Back River" folk were still living on the edge of their tribes, now on the edge of town, in squalid shacks, too poor to own decent cookware.

Christmas was almost upon us at Baker Lake, and I was already starting to feel sorry for myself. The previous year, I had spent Christmas at a remote fur-trading outpost called Ogoki with two unbathed, unshaven, and completely bushed Newfoundlanders. There was no way I was going to have another Christmas like that one. Since I was the guy who ordered all of the supplies for the Hudson's Bay store, I had many business connections in the south, and I knew enough pilots to get just about anything smuggled into the community.

I had promised myself a Christmas tree that year, and even though I was a thousand kilometres from the nearest tree, I had the savvy required to have one flown in.

My produce supplier was to cleverly disguise my tree as a large item of produce and slip it into our weekly cargo shipment of freshies. The task of disguising the tree was as challenging as trying to gift-wrap a hockey stick and did not go over very well with the cargo loadmaster at the airline. A well-placed bottle of Scotch overcame his objections, and I was assured the tree would be delivered on or before Christmas Eve.

On the morning of Christmas Eve, the DC3 aircraft, trying to beat deteriorating weather, arrived two days late and several hours ahead of schedule. Such surprises were quite common in the Arctic, but I had been caught off guard. Doug, the store manager, was rousted from his bed at 5 AM. The two cranky pilots had forgotten to radio ahead for some Company boys to unload the aircraft.

I awoke to the distinctive sound of an ancient DC3 struggling for altitude and attempting to shear the shingles off my house as if to say, "Merry Christmas, nice knowing you, Christmas Boy." It took me less than two minutes to scramble into my clothes and get over to the store.

Somehow, Doug had already unloaded the truck and was attempting to open a rather large, mysteriously cone-shaped box of produce. Just as flight schedule changes were common, freight bumping was also quite a common occurrence, and Doug's much-awaited boxes of Christmas cheer had been bumped to make room for my tree.

By 9 AM when the store opened for the last day of shopping before Christmas, I was reading the newly revised duty roster, which now had me working all day and again on Boxing Day. In fact, I was scheduled to work all store hours of every day, forever.

It cheered me somewhat to notice the crowd gathering around the freshly decorated Christmas tree, which had suddenly appeared in the front window of the store. The Inuit were curious folks and most had never seen a real tree. I overheard one elder telling several children that he had never been to the south because it must stink down there. Some children laughed as if they did not believe him, causing the old man to snap off a branch, which was sniffed enthusiastically as it was passed around the now crowded store. I stepped into the back of the store, only for a minute, to wheel out the newly arrived fresh produce. When I returned to the front of the store, the crowd of Inuit was gone and so was my tree. In its place stood a broom handle that was once a Scotch pine, with a heap of tattered decorations at its base. I sighed and began working as shoppers came and went and the excitement grew in anticipation of the announcement of the

This type of house was called a "matchbox." They were the first homes built for the Inuit by the government. Several matchboxes were built in each community. They were still in use during my time in the north. This was Hughie's house. If it looks tiny, that is because tiny houses were easier to heat. (Baker Lake, NU, 1980)

winner of the Bay's Christmas contest.

Earlier in the week, I had convinced the manager that a big Christmas contest could well stimulate the local folks to do their Christmas shopping with us instead of with the Sears mail-order catalogue. We offered a new fourteen-inch colour TV as a draw prize. The contest idea worked since television was new to Baker Lake; not many people had a set in their home. The draw was to be held at closing time on Christmas Eve. By the end of the day, the excitement was fairly palpable.

I worked hard all day and tried to keep my mind off the fact that it was Christmas and here I was, unbathed, unshaven, and feeling quite bushed. I noticed that someone had now made off with the broom handle that was once my tree. Our only cashier had gone for lunch and not returned, so I was now responsible for running the busy checkout until closing time. As 5 PM approached, I served my last customer, who purchased four oranges, a roll of twine, and four yards of calico fabric. His name was Hughie. I did not know his last name.

He was a quiet and sad fellow whom I had not often seen out and about in the community. He was a Pot and certainly looked the part; he was wearing an ill-fitting parka, which was stained with stove oil, and a pair of oilcloth kamiks through which you could tell the colour of his socks. Hughie paid for his purchase with a jar of pennies, which he had produced from the only untorn pocket in his coat.

The store had begun to fill with people in anticipation of the big Christmas draw; many were now laughing loudly and watching Hughie as he asked me to count out the pennies. I suddenly realized he could not count them himself. Having bagged Hughie's purchases, I passed him his receipt on which I had instructed him to write his name and to place it in the draw box for the TV.

He said, "No thanks" and fled the store without daring to raise his face and look anyone in the eye. After all, he was a Pot: he should not have been there in the first place. As the door swung closed, the crowd roared with laughter as someone pointed out that Pots did not know how to write their names. Embarrassed, I scribbled Hughie's name on his receipt and stuffed it into the draw box. Doug announced that the draw would be in five minutes. The announcement started a flurry of small purchases that produced sales receipts, which could be entered in the draw.

When draw time arrived, Doug opened the draw box and thoroughly scrambled all of the receipts. He then called upon the Anglican minister to reach in and select the winning person's receipt. I looked around the store and noticed that we could not have possibly squeezed another person into the building.

Everyone seemed to be holding his or her breath. Five children were standing in the front window where my tree used to stand, all with eyes as big as snowballs.

The minister said something very serious in Inuktitut and all were nodding their heads in agreement. It had been decided that an elder should make the draw. Jessie was pushed forward and almost seemed reluctant to have been given such an honour.

Jessie, who was a member of the Order of Canada, was the most respected elder in the community. She resembled the Ukrainian babushkas who used to drag kids home by the ear in my old neighbourhood. All went quiet as Jessie again mixed up the tangle of paper in the draw box.

Reaching deeply into the box that was held high above her 1.3 metres of height, Jessie pulled out a small crumpled receipt and passed it to the minister. With a warm smile, the minister announced in Inuktitut, "The winner is ... Hughie!" Silence. After a couple of uncomfortable moments, people started whispering and gesturing to one another. Doug and the minister were summoned into the midst of the crowd, which seemed to be fanning itself into a mini-riot. Sharp words were exchanged between the minister and several of the Inuit contest entrants. The red-faced minister stormed out of the store. Doug returned to his previous position beside me and in front of the now angry crowd. "They say they don't think a Pot should win, and they are pointing out that there are no Pots in the store so they would never know anyway because no one talks to them." Doug looked to me as if I had the wisdom to solve the dilemma. "Let's do what is right," I whispered to Doug. He agreed.

"Hughie wins the TV," Doug yelled out. "You take care of closing up. I'll see you on Boxing Day," he said, and out the door he went.

It took me a good hour to clear the store, and when everyone was out and the door was locked, I took a minute to survey the scene. The store was practically destroyed, but I figured I could clean it on Boxing Day. The TV was still sitting on its perch, plugged in, and the *Happy Days* theme song was just beginning to play on CBC, which was the only channel available.

It suddenly occurred to me that Hughie had no phone, and I had no way of letting him know that he had won. It only seemed fair to drop the TV off at his place, but Doug had taken the truck and was nowhere to be found. I packed the TV back into its box and flipped off the lights to head home for another disappointing Christmas.

In the darkened store, I sat down for a minute and started to feel sorry for myself again. I just could not believe that I was about to spend another Christmas, alone, in the darkest and coldest of Arctic winters, without a tree. I felt as if I needed to cry, but I held back with one thought. I began to wonder what kind of Christmas Hughie was having. Whatever kind of Christmas he and his family were having, I became sure that winning a TV would make it a better one.

Fifteen minutes later, I was humping a large, heavy, gift-wrapped box through the Arctic darkness in search of Hughie's shack somewhere between the edge of town and the tundra.

Twice I had to stop at people's houses and ask for directions. Everyone seemed to know what was in the box and where I was taking it. It was 8 PM on Christmas Eve, and I was rapping on the door of a tiny plywood shack, which seemed to be sitting alone in the darkness, half-buried by snow.

Hughie answered the door with a big smile and invited me in. I struggled inside with the box; Hughie was too stunned at the sight of me to remember to help. I was offered a seat, one of two in the two-room shack.

There was a single window with no curtain; the wind could be heard through the large crack between the glass and its frame. The walls were plain plywood, stained with soot, and, no doubt, had never felt the touch of a paintbrush. There was an oil-burning stove on one side of the room and on the other side, a small kitchen table, circa 1950, with two un-upholstered upholstered chairs. At our feet sat a dirty-faced, brown-eyed cherub on a porcelain potty, smiling at me while grunting and straining with great effort. In the other room were two single mattresses lying on the floor, each with a soiled sleeping bag and a yellowed, stained pillow. On one mattress, Hughie's wife sat with three children, each with a joyous face as they had just received their Christmas gift … an orange.

Mrs. Hughie was playing a game wherein she peeled each child's orange, slowly and carefully so that the orange shed its skin in one curly piece. In the far corner was a "honey bucket," a crude toilet that had been sectioned off from the rest of the room with a newly made calico curtain hanging on a string that was tacked into the walls.

I heard a particularly loud grunt and a subsequent plop, and Hughie reached down to stroke the hair of the little guy who was doing his business on the potty. I suddenly felt ashamed, terribly uncomfortable, and ready to dart from the house. Hughie asked me how my Christmas was going as his wife finished peeling the last orange and passed it back to her waiting child.

I was not able to say much as the gaseous product of his son's efforts had now reached my nostrils. "It's going good, Hughie. I can't stay long, I've got to be going home … you know how it is." Hughie smiled and nodded.

"Are you taking home that present for someone?" Hughie inquired.

"You won the draw at the Bay, Hughie. This TV is yours." Hughie broke into a semi-toothless smile. Hughie's wife came out of the other room, and among the three of us, we unwrapped the box and set the TV on the only piece of furniture they had, the table.

As Hughie's tiny family gathered around the TV, the room took on a blue glow from the picture tube. Previously, the house had been illuminated by two bare bulbs, which hung from the stained plywood ceiling. I shook Hughie's hand and wished him and his family a merry Christmas. Hughie snatched his dirty parka from a nail next to the door. "I'll walk you home."

I did not see any other coats hanging in the house and could not help but wonder if Hughie's wife or children were able to leave the house in winter if they had only one coat to wear among all of them.

As we walked back to my staff house, we said little. But, just as we passed the store, Hughie said, "You know, this is the second time I have been very lucky at Christmas."

There had been a tuberculosis epidemic in Baker Lake and his elder brother, his hero, had been flown out to a place called "Hamilton." Hughie missed his brother terribly, especially when Christmas arrived. On Christmas Eve, Hughie was in the Bay store with his dad when he spotted something unusual lying on the floor.

Hughie had picked it up, looking about him to see if anyone had seen what he had found; quickly he tucked the tiny treasure into his mitten. He said nothing to anyone about what he had found as he was not exactly sure what it was, but he knew it must be valuable. As the family sat in their tent, by the light of their kerosene lamp, Hughie worked up the courage to show everyone what he had found. They all gasped as he held it out in his hand.

Hughie's father laughed as he saw that Hughie had, in fact, found an unused postage stamp. A story was then told, as people who have nothing but one another and time on their hands tell stories. "If you put the stamp on paper, the white people who fly the planes will take the paper anywhere in the world, to whomever you want." Hughie proudly held his stamp and walked around the tent so that all could see the jewel that he had found.

On Christmas Day, Hughie woke up before everyone else and raced over to see the RCMP officer's wife. She had been teaching Hughie words in English and he had been teaching her Inuktitut. He told her of how he had come to be the owner of a postage stamp. The kind woman asked Hughie what he was going to do with his treasure. Hughie then asked her if she could put it on a paper and give it to a pilot to bring to his brother, who was in a place called Hamilton, and put words on the paper to tell him to come home.

Teary eyed, they worked together on a letter, sealed it in an envelope, and the woman promised to give it to a pilot, which she did.

By this point in Hughie's story we had arrived at my house and I asked Hughie if he would like to come in and warm up for awhile. He politely declined and said, "So, you see, Christmas is a very lucky time for me." I agreed and wished Hughie a merry Christmas.

Just as he turned to leave, I had to ask him, "Hughie, your letter to your brother … did he ever write you back?"

"No," he said. "Sometimes the pilots can't find people, or maybe they are unable to fly to where they are because of the weather. I haven't heard back from him yet."

TWO-GOAT WATCH

Spring had arrived late that year, and I quietly wondered if the hull of Don's old boat would take the pounding it was getting as it struck loose-floating pans of ice. Don looked confident, though, and that put me at ease. I couldn't imagine this man doing anything other than what he was doing at the moment.

The Gentlemen and Adventurers of England Trading into Hudson Bay had contracted Don and his boat, *Windjammer*, to convey me along with a load of groceries and three bags of mail to its Lac Seul Post. The map had shown the small fur-trading outpost set on a point of land jutting into the Lac Seul waterway, which extends north one hundred and fifty kilometres from Sioux Lookout to Ear Falls. I'd read a bit about the history of the

My friend David Starrat, grandson of aviation pioneer Robert W. Starrat, is helping me to corral the company goats. The goats were frequently spotted by deer hunters and had many a close call. David held the goats while I spray-painted each with "Property of HBC" stencils on both sides, using bright red spray paint. The "deer" made it through hunting season with flying colours, so to speak. (Lac Seul Post, ON, 1981)

area when it was one of the focuses of the trade wars between the North West Company and the Hudson's Bay Company. It seems the HBC manager liquored up some of the local trappers and got them riled by telling them the North West Company manager had called them a bunch of sissies. The resulting decapitation served to eliminate the difficulties that seem to arise whenever commercial competition rears its ugly head in the bush.

"Are we almost there?" I asked.

Don turned and looked at me with surprise. "I don't know,

but when we get there, we'll be halfway." It occurred to me that Don was either very wise or very stupid. At that moment, the *Windjammer* hit a deadhead, killing the engine and tossing me headfirst into a case of Wonder Bread. The old bushman leaned over the stern, calmly inspected the prop, removed the cowling from the inboard motor, and peered down into the compartment.

"Looks all right. Turn the key and see if she starts." *Click. Click. Click.* "No luck. I guess we'll have to paddle the rest of the way." It probably wasn't the best time to show that this Toronto high school graduate knew his way around the woods. Don tinkered with the engine for several moments, ignoring my comments. Suddenly, amidst aspersions hurled at the Swedish bastards who had built the Volvo inboard, the engine came back to life and we were off.

I noticed a small gash on Don's wrist where he had smashed his watch while working on the engine. Don briefly inspected its shattered crystal and one missing hand, then silently removed it and flung it overboard. The sun burned high in the sky and I listened to the pat, pat, pat of the bow skimming across the waves. Lac Seul would be my first posting as manager.

The *Windjammer* swung around a clump of submerged stumps and pushed her way past an ice patch shimmering in the noonday sun like a swath of moonlight on a silent lake. There, boldly perched on a southward slope, were red-shingled, white-washed buildings surrounded by meadow and beach, an oasis. Red pines two feet in girth towered against the primitive bush; fence posts holding the wilderness out, holding civilization in. Don swung the *Windjammer* into dock, a manoeuvre he no doubt had done countless times. He leapt overboard and tied us in.

I began to toss the cargo to Don while he threw it onto a small trailer. A slow-moving fellow slouched on a forty-five gallon fuel drum and watched us work as he rolled a smoke. "That's Joe Trout. He's so lazy he'd chop a tree down just so he could sit on the stump and watch you work," said Don. We finished unloading and walked up the dock.

I found myself walking quickly. I'm not sure if I was hurrying toward the store or away from Joe. He was now struggling to light his smoke while still perched on the fuel drum. As we approached the store, the racket of a small lawn tractor came bouncing off the side of the warehouse. A man who must have weighed two hundred kilos was cutting the grass on the west meadow. The engine noise had allowed us to arrive unnoticed. The tractor swerved, retracted its cutting blade, and swung from its path to intercept us at the front of the store. The engine of the tractor still droned as if it were straining not from the effort of cutting grass, but from carrying the bulk of the mystery tractor driver.

"That's Doug," Don pointed out. "He's fat." I took comfort in knowing that I wasn't the only person present with a penchant for stating the obvious.

Doug disembarked from the tiny tractor and offered his sweaty, stubby-fingered hand. "Hi, I'm Doug," he bellowed. No doubt his ears were still ringing from the engine noise. "You must be my replacement."

"This is John. He's from Toronto." Don tended to cram as much information into an introduction as possible.

The path to the house was well worn from multiple tractor trips between the house and the store. Doug walked slowly, ten steps behind us and just out of earshot. "Doug doesn't like walking much," Don said. "In winter he rides a Ski-Doo between the house and the store."

The house was a post–Second World War design with four bedrooms, gaping windows, and poorly insulated walls. "Have a seat," Doug said. "I've got some ice cream."

We chatted comfortably about the post and my duties, Doug's answers to my questions slurped out between heaping mouthfuls of maple walnut ice cream. Then Doug waddled back to the tractor to pick up the trailer load of freight. Wondering what time it was, Don strolled back to the beach with me tagging along. In the distance we could see Doug tumbling off the tractor to pursue Joe Trout, who had opened the mailbags and was dumping the contents onto the beach for sorting. That was a waste of time, as I was later to learn that Joe couldn't read.

As Don boarded the *Windjammer,* I heard him cussing. A high-flying gull had dropped its load on the driver's seat and left a poop-streamer across the centre of the windshield. "Damned welfare birds!" Before I could offer to run up to the store to get a rag, Don rang out, "Hey, Joe, I'll give you a ride over to Kejick Bay. Hop in. You drive. I'll see you guys in a couple of days." Happy to be offered such an honour, Joe eagerly jumped into the driver's seat. In a flush of foam and spray, they were off.

Lac Seul, or Lonely Lake, was an untended garden. Nature threatened constantly to return the post to sage grass, alders, and hazel brush. Doug had worked out a daily routine to keep the forces of nature at bay. "When we're out of fur-trading season, your time is spent on upkeep of the post. Whitewash the buildings, maintain the generator, and keep the grass and bush cut back." Two hours a day were to be spent on the lawn tractor and weeks cutting brush. After more discussion and another quart of ice cream, we returned to the house, where I was shown my room. I crawled into my narrow bunk and lay very still, tired from my long journey, listening for all of the sounds one hears on the first night in a strange place. Red-tailed squirrels scolded one another in the distance. Birds chattered in the eavestroughs. A soft summer wind sighed through the red pines, and with the sound of warm waves surrounding me, I fell asleep.

Morning snuck up on me. I had planned to get up before Doug set out on his arduous forty-six-metre tractor journey to the store, but I was too late. Off he went, the tractor engine again straining under its burden. As I looked out the grimy kitchen window, Don was pulling up to the dock in the *Windjammer.*

The night before, he had said he would be back in a couple of days. This was one of many lessons about the north that I was to learn from Don. Watches and calendars have little meaning up here. Time and language become vague; "a couple of days" can mean two days, two weeks, two hours, or not at all.

"Let's get unloaded!" Don shouted. "I've got another trip to make today." When Don wanted things done, they got done. He based his life on two simple philosophies: If you want something done, do it yourself; and, avoid people who are educated beyond their intelligence.

When the boat was unloaded and Don came up to the post, I noticed a white patch of skin on his arm where his watch used to be. My first day on the job, I couldn't resist trying to sell Don a new watch. "Well, let's see what you've got. I'm in a hurry." I showed him the watches in stock and Don spotted the same model as the one he had lost the previous day. "How much for that one?"

"Forty-nine ninety-five, but for you, thirty bucks." I could tell Doug was not impressed that I was discounting his merchandise before we had a chance to change management and do an inventory count. Wise man that he was, Don knew a good deal when he saw one.

"Sold."

Don pulled the watch out of its package, slapped it on his wrist, and slipped out the door all in one motion.

"Good going, salesman!" Doug lamented. "Don never carries cash. You can kiss that thirty bucks goodbye!"

Following Don's broad strides down to the dock, I was stuck for a way to ask him to pay without offending him. Since he'd said he was coming back that afternoon, I decided to ask to go into town with him and somehow slip into the conversation that I needed to be paid for the watch.

Don stood all the way back to town, a position affording a better view of the potential hazards that lay ahead. No doubt our collision with the deadhead the previous day was still fresh in his mind. We pulled out into the open water and choppy waves of the bay where Don's family had operated a seaplane base for many years. Shortly we bore down on the town of Hudson, its wooden buildings all but obscured by the thick growth of cedars that lined the shore.

"So what do you think of the post?" Don asked.

"So far so good," I said. This looked like an opportunity to slip in a hint about the thirty dollars. "Don," I ventured, "I think I forgot my wallet. I was hoping to pick up a few things while we're here."

"Don't worry about it," Don said. "I never carry cash and I've always done just fine without it."

I resigned myself to paying for the watch and decided to drop the matter forever. As we tied up the boat, Don further probed my feelings about my new posting, then offered, "The only hard part seems to be all of the time you have to waste cutting grass." He paused for a moment, drawing a rough finger across his chin. "What you need is a goat." Humouring him, I agreed that it was a great idea, but where would one find a goat in northern Ontario? We parted ways agreeing to meet back at the dock in "a couple of hours."

The morning passed slowly and it looked as if we were going to have our first really warm day of spring. I finished my errands and waited on the dock for more than an hour. I was amused that Don was late, even though he had a new watch.

On my left stood the warehouse, from which we would later be loading the boat. I glanced to my right toward the fuel depot and there, to my surprise, sat Joe Trout on a drum of aviation fuel, rolling a smoke. Joe was such a creature of habit. Suddenly he slid off the drum and strolled over to the dock, where Don had pulled up in an old Ford pickup. In the box of the truck stood a pair of goats, which he was trying to untie and coax to step off the tailgate. His attention caught, Joe actually exerted himself to help offload the two strange-looking deer that Don had captured.

As Don and Joe fumbled down the walkway with the doltish looking creatures, I asked, "How much?"

"Thirty dollars," Don boasted. "The guy wanted fifty bucks each for them. I talked him down."

Don extended his palm, giving me the opportunity to reimburse him. I pretended I didn't notice his hand and concentrated on the goats. What ridiculous creatures, knobby and rough-calloused knees, mousy fur, and those eyes, which denoted irritable stupidity. How would we ever handle these fidgety creatures on a two-hour boat trip? Don's keen analytical mind had already been at work on the problem. He tossed the goats into the boat, then, keeping them standing, he tied their horns to a bulkhead. Don must have understood something of goat psychology. For the duration of the trip they didn't move or make a sound.

Bringing Joe along hadn't been necessary, or useful for that matter. Joe spent the trip trying to roll a smoke in the wind, looking up occasionally to stare longingly at the goats, no doubt wondering if they would be as tasty as venison. A half-hour out of Kejick Bay, Don smelled smoke. He stopped the engine and sprinted to the engine compartment. As he lifted the cowling from the engine, a wisp of smoke curled up, smelling of burnt plastic. Unknown to us, the goats had been dropping copious quantities of organic jelly beans that the vibration of the engine had danced back to the bilge pump. The pump had become blocked and had melted itself from its mounting.

"Damned goats! Damned Swedish Volvo bastards!" Don was upset.

Restarting the engine, we continued on our silent way. The afternoon had grown unbearably hot and the goats had started to sweat. As we docked at Lac Seul post, Don cut the goats free and sent them trotting off to the inviting grass of the west meadow. Don's anger had not yet abated. He untied the *Windjammer* and rudely throttled away, cursing loudly about Swedish bastards and damned goats as he rounded the point. I watched him dodge the submerged stumps, breaking his concentration briefly to glance at his watch.

Later that evening I learned that Don had struck a deadhead two miles from home. Without a bilge pump, the *Windjammer* sank quickly in a swirl of organic jelly beans. Don made it to shore and in a cloud of curses flung a sacrifice to the deep.

To this day, the *Windjammer* lies on the bottom of Lac Seul, right beside Don's brand new two-goat watch.

SECOND BEAR OVER

Despite the beautiful and wondrous surroundings of Lac Seul Post in winter, spring was always a welcome sight. By then, the lake ice would have rotted into "ice candles," which sounded like wind chimes as they swirled and bobbed in the gentle waves that brushed the shoreline of the calm lake. The Hudson's Bay Company had owned the island for many years. The forest had never been logged there, giving the island a distinctive skyline of mature red pines, each of which was so thick you couldn't wrap your arms around it.

I had heard from the people of Kejick Bay that wildlife frequently swam over to the island outpost and refused to leave. As a result, I had been asked by many of the trappers to summon them if a bear or moose were to become marooned there. What they had in mind was not a rescue but an easy hunt and quick lunch provided by my uninvited guests.

The local folks had already played many practical jokes on me and had grown quite fond of teasing their very young factor. As a result, I did not believe that a bear or moose would take the time to swim over to this tiny island when they had access to all the bush out there. However, while doing my spring maintenance one clear morning, which included whitewashing the generator shack, I heard a sharp "crack" coming from the direction of the trading post. I ran down to the beach to see what was unfolding and found one of my customers skinning out a black bear that had swum across the lake to do his shopping at the post. I guess they weren't pulling my leg on this one.

A few weeks later, Ed came running into the post, out of breath and out of tobacco. Ed was once the "post servant" for Lac Seul Post but was now retired. He lived on the far end of the island in a tiny log cabin that had been provided for him by the company many years ago. The Bay owned the land and the shack. As a reward for services rendered over many years, Ed was allowed to stay in the shack until he died or chose to move away. He was the only neighbour I had on the island other than the visiting wildlife.

"A bear swam over last night and wrecked my place!"

"That's the second bear over," I pointed out to Ed. "Why did he go after your place?"

"I was hanging moose meat to dry," said Ed. "I had meat all over the place."

I grabbed my rifle. It was a .30-.30, not a bad bush gun, but I didn't know if it could take down a bear. By the time we got to Ed's shack, the bear had gone and had left no tracks. The cabin was a mess. I offered to help Ed clean things up, but he refused and asked to be left alone. Ed seemed to be taking the bear attack rather personally. I suppose I would have been just as upset if a bear had eaten all my winter provisions. I cautiously walked back to the post, hoping that I wouldn't run into the bear on the trail.

Two nights later, our furry friend reappeared; he had probably finished digesting Ed's moose. I had just pulled back the living room curtains in the staff house to let in a little more light. There, with his nose pressed against the window, was Ed's bear, looking me right in the eye. I was startled, and I fumbled with the box of .30-.30 shells as I went out the back door and tried to flank the cheeky bruin. Once again, he was gone.

I took my rifle and climbed up onto the roof of the staff house to see if I could spot the marauding beast. Nothing. I turned to go back down the ladder and there he was, standing on his back legs, holding the ladder for me. I guess he didn't want me to fall off the roof, as he did not desire bruised meat for supper. I hit him in the chest three times before I realized that I had loaded "hard-nosed" shells into my gun, which hurt him but did not bring him down. The wounded bear made for the woods just as Ed appeared to see what was going on.

"Did you get him?" Ed asked.

"I hit him three times, but he wouldn't stay down," I complained.

"We can't leave a wounded bear out there," Ed said. "I have a floodlight at the cabin; I'll get it and we'll track him to finish him off."

When Ed returned fifteen minutes later, it was completely dark. The "floodlight" turned out to be a regular old flashlight that cast such a weak light that a birthday candle would have done a better job. Ed also had a rifle that looked older than he was.

"Let's get the son of a bitch!" Ed called out as he charged into the woods. "He wrecked my place!"

There was nothing I could say to Ed to convince him not to go into the bush after dark to track a wounded bear that had no fear of man. I was sure that if the bear ate this old guy, I'd be in a lot of trouble. Also, I didn't think it would be a good idea to lose one of my customers. I followed Ed into the bush, asking him to stay where he was until I caught up to him. Ed's floodlight had just about piddled out by the time I reached him.

"Let's get out of here, Ed. This is nuts," I pleaded.

Ed took a step backward and tripped over the bear's leg.

"Shine the light on him, Ed!" I yelled.

Ed dropped the flashlight as he fumbled to find his ammunition. It is beyond me why a person of Ed's years would have followed a wounded bear into the woods with his only bullet in his shirt pocket and not in his rifle. Ed grabbed his "floodlight" and fired at the bear, which was now standing on its back legs, roaring, swinging at us, and spitting blood. Ed's *only bullet* found the bear's foot. I pushed Ed behind me and emptied my gun into the bear, dropping it instantly. With the "floodlight" now gone and Ed's arsenal spent, we walked back out to the beach.

The first customers at the post the following morning asked if I had heard shooting the previous night. I told them what had happened and the family asked if they could have the bear.

I told them, "If you can find it, it's yours."

As I helped the family carry their supplies to the dock, Ed emerged from the bush with several young men from the reserve. They were dragging the bear out of the woods to see if the hide or meat was salvageable. The chief was with them, and he was shaking his head and laughing at Ed.

All the people at the post took a quick look at the bear and left it where it lay.

"Doesn't anyone want the hide or meat?" I asked the chief.

"That hide would only be useful as a screen door," he jested. "How many times did you shoot that thing?"

"I think we hit it about eleven times altogether," I replied sheepishly.

"That bear died of lead poisoning," said the chief with a straight face. "No one will be wanting any of that meat."

After every single person from the reserve had come over to the post to hear about the fatal confrontation between man and beast and to view the resulting carnage, I found myself alone with my furry nemesis. Both the pelt and the meat were ruined; no one on the reserve would take me up on the offer of a free bear feast. The only option left to me was to offer the poor guy a decent burial, which turned out to be a bigger job than I had imagined. I wish there had been a better way to deal with the situation. It was a terrible waste and made me acutely aware of how much I did not know about the environment in which I had chosen to live.

MR. JAKE

It was the early eighties and the fur trade had just about dried up
when I arrived in Kugluktuk to take over the outpost, which had
been operating there for more than fifty years. At the time, the
HBC was still operating its outpost general stores all across Canada's
north, selling pots, pans, traps, and groceries, just as it had for three
hundred years. And, of course, the company still traded for furs
with Canada's aboriginal peoples. Lesson number one at the
Hudson's Bay Company was "The customer is always right."
Never did I see this maxim carried out quite as fully, or to such
interesting effect, as at the Kugluktuk post.

   As post manager I was required at least to attempt to learn
the local dialect, Inuktitut. However, even though I had learned

to speak some Cree and Ojibwa the previous year at Lac Seul in northern Ontario, Inuktitut continued to elude me. Kugluktuk was way above the Arctic Circle, and I had begun to forget what a tree looked like. I certainly liked the fishing and was beginning to enjoy my relationship with the Inuit who resided there. Well, most of them anyway. As with every rule, there is always an exception. The exception in Kugluktuk was a rather unconventional old man named Jake.

Jake seemed to break all the rules that determine "Eskimoness." He was tall and wiry, his face weather-beaten and leathery. For an old guy he certainly had nice teeth, and his hands looked as if he were wearing a pair of baseball mitts. Jake enjoyed the status of elder and also of master hunter, trapper, and marksman. For some reason, Jake would never make the effort to communicate directly with me. Though he looked me straight in the eye at all times, he always had a tiny sidekick with him who translated on his behalf.

When I had first arrived in Kugluktuk and was trying to conduct business with Jake, I asked his sidekick what his name was. The young boy indicated his name was also Jake, which led me to assume that Jake's companion was his grandson. It soon became apparent, however, that each time Jake visited the store he had a different youngster with him. In every instance I would ask the little boy what his name was, and he would always enthusiastically respond that his name was also Jake. It seemed against the odds that the small community of Kugluktuk should have so many Jakes. I made some discreet inquiries.

It seemed that each morning Jake would enter the local school and borrow a youngster to be his protegé and translator for the day. Jake promptly instructed the draftee that his name would be "Jake" for the duration of his employment. I suppose Jake felt that any young man should feel honoured to be a Jake-in-training, even if it were just for one day. Mrs. Humphries' Grade four class's grade-point average was decimated each year as her class became populated by a disproportionate number of Jakes.

Jake always carried a Swiss Army knife. Apparently, the knife had been a gift from one of my predecessors. The story was that Jake was such an exceptional hunter and trapper that all stood in overwhelming wonder of him, including the *kadloonatt*, or white people, of the community. As a result of Jake's renown, his ego had become so inflated that you couldn't fit it through the door-way of the average igloo. It was with that knife that Jake was to challenge all that was retail as I knew it.

Each day, upon entering the store, Jake would give his assis-tant a cardboard box and instructions to follow him as he shopped. The Swiss Army knife was then produced, and one of its three hundred and twenty-one blades would be flipped open to begin the shopping excursion. If Jake were shopping for breakfast, he would make his first stop at the dairy case. There, he would cut an inch of butter off the end of a pound and carefully return the rest to the case for the next customer. From there he would proceed to the meat counter, where, with a slash of his blade he would remove three strips of bacon from a package. Two tea bags would then be plucked from their homes; four slices of bread raided from a loaf; and finally, a handful of sugar would be tapped off from a two-kilo bag. While Jake shopped, little Jake would follow, placing the needed commodities into the box.

Jake bought only what he needed.

Jake would terminate his shopping excursion at the front checkout, where little Jake would initiate negotiations for Jake's breakfast needs. Needless to say, the annoyed and panicky cashier would then summon me. I had learned over the months just to work with Jake, as his arguments for shopping that way were infi-nitely practical, solidly logical, and besides, he was as stubborn as a rusty leghold trap.

Spring had arrived and the daylight had returned as I made my way to the store to open for the day. Waiting outside the front doors for me was Jake. A new Jake, who was clearly no older than seven, was trailing him. On inquiry, I discovered that Mrs. Humphries had taken her room full of Grade four Jakes on a field trip. The Grade two class convened right next door, and since

Jake was in a hurry he had drafted a Jake from the minor leagues.

I twirled the lock and entered the darkened store with the two Jakes hot on my heels.

"Jake wants to buy bullets," the first-round draft choice sang out. "It's spring and the caribou are close to town."

Big Jake made his way to the ammunition and immediately cut the box open to remove three shells. Jake was still using his First World War .303 Lee Enfield rifle, and it held only three bullets.

"Come on, Jake," I heard myself whine. "This is getting ridiculous!" Big Jake promptly rebuffed me with a tirade of sounds I had never heard before. "What did he just call me?" I asked little Jake.

"He said he was offering twenty-five cents for each bullet. He is in a hurry and he has decided he is not going to pay any tax today either."

It was the shortest negotiation in Inuit history as Jake dropped three quarters onto the counter, asked for a bag, and sprinted out the door faster than little Jake could follow. I decided to take the rest of the day off as I felt I had already put in a whole day's work.

The next day, as I approached the store, I could see a lone figure waiting at the front door. It was Jake, grinning from ear to ear, wearing bloodied boots that indicated success on his hunt the previous day. He looked naked without a little Jake backing him up. I was thinking that without translation, how bad could his visit possibly be? As I unlocked the door, Jake pointed to his snowmobile and komatik sled, which had a rather unfortunate-looking caribou roped onto it.

"Way to go, Jake," I said.

Jake smiled and followed me into the store. I turned on the lights and came back to the front checkout to see what Jake needed for breakfast. I was stunned to silence as Jake placed two bullets on the counter and growled, "Refund."

I knew I did not stand a chance and dropped two quarters into his gnarly fingers. Jake turned from me, pulled out his Swiss Army knife, and headed to the frozen food section.

SEAL HOLES AND
LONG JOHNS

There always seemed to be a threshold I would cross wherein an arctic community would forget that I was the new guy in town, and I would no longer stand out as being suspicious or foreign. The Inuit of the Canadian Arctic have a maxim that states: "White people come from the south, stay a week, and write a pamphlet; stay a month and write a book." I always looked forward to blending into a community, no longer remembering that I had once lived another way, the Inuit forgetting that I was amongst them. It was then that both the Inuit and I were at our best and then that I best experienced the beauty and harmony of the north and its people, unencumbered by expectations or preconceptions.

After four years of operating the Hudson's Bay Company's outpost stores, I felt there was little left that I had not experienced. However, my Inuit employees, though earnest and well meaning, occasionally came up with rationales and concepts that defied my understanding. That was certainly the case when I arrived in the community of Kugluktuk, on the Arctic coast on the Coronation Gulf.

When a new Bay manager arrived in a community, the first order of business was always an inventory. At Kugluktuk, I assembled ten inventory crews, each consisting of a counter/caller and a recorder who wrote the figures on the inventory sheets. As I passed around the pens, clipboards, and inventory sheets, my crew assured me that they were all veteran inventory takers and that a review of procedure was not necessary. Being a veteran myself, I decided we would review the procedure anyway. The morning passed quickly and I was pleased with the rapid progress my counters were making. Before long, it was time to break for lunch and I dismissed my jovial bunch with a stern request for a prompt return after lunch.

I felt it would be advantageous to spot check the inventory sheets while the store was vacant. The inventory sheets seemed to be in good order, with one glaring exception. In the box that read "inventory count," which should contain numerical values only, such as "12" cans of beans or "7" bags of sugar, the word "many" had been used whenever there were more than a dozen or so of any particular item. The Inuit, who are infinitely more practical than I, were conducting an inventory in order to make sure there was enough of everything. Apparently, "many" indicated "enough," and therefore one did not need to waste one's time actually counting an item of which there was plenty. It all makes sense, I suppose. At the same time, I found myself having to teach my employees many tasks that I thought of as simple; it was often tedious and time-consuming as I showed them another way of seeing the world.

The Copper Eskimos, as the great explorer Samuel Hearne had named them, were at their best when out on the land. It was on the land where I found myself to be the student, my Inuit friends patiently teaching me to see things in another way. When on the barren lands, the simplest of tasks became tedious and time-consuming as this wide-eyed Hudson's Bay man learned the ropes. My favourite mentor at Kugluktuk was a quiet and patient middle-aged man named Frank, whose wife worked in the store. Frank's family had decided to take me under their wing.

One glorious spring day, just as the sun had begun to come back to us, Frank appeared at my door dressed in caribou skins and grinning from ear to ear. "Let's go seal hunting," he said. "Dress warmly and I will be back to get you. I'm going to get some gas." Then, without waiting for a response, he was gone.

I dressed in many layers, as I did not have a set of caribou skins of my own. When I was satisfied that I would be warm, I could hardly move and found that I could not rest my arms at my sides. I had not worn long johns since I was a kid, and I was now reminded why. I don't know who designed the thermal gotchies, but the crotch hung to my knees and the cuffs on the legs seemed to have been designed to cut off the circulation at my extremities. The overall effect caused me to walk as if I had a most unfortunate case of diaper rash.

Frank returned in short order and did not even slow down as he signalled for me to jump onto his komatik sled. I landed ungracefully on the sled with a great thud and heard Frank's snowmobile engine begin to labour under the additional weight. I was hoping no one had seen me landing like a sack of potatoes; I sure didn't feel very dignified as I hung on for dear life.

Periodically, Frank would slow down and point to various items of interest, and I would nod enthusiastically. I had absolutely no idea what he was pointing at, as all I could see was white. We were out on the sea ice, under a glaring sun; I could not even ascertain the horizon let alone spot the indigenous wildlife. All I knew for sure was: if I fell off this sled and Frank couldn't find me, I was a dead man.

After what seemed like hours, Frank stopped his machine and came back to see how I was doing. It seemed like a good time to take a personal inventory. I was sure I was bleeding from the kidneys as the sled had been bucking like a drunken rodeo bull. I no longer had any feeling in my hands or feet, not because I was cold, but from gripping the sled in sheer terror. My bladder was about to burst, but I had no idea how I was going to relieve myself, as the opening in my long johns was not aligned with the semi-frozen equipment required to do the job. Otherwise, I was intact and ready to do harm to any seal careless enough to cross my path.

Frank pointed out that we were now in an area where seals came up through holes in the ice and sunned themselves. If we spotted one, we would shoot it, butcher it on the ice, and head home for the big feast. He made it sound so simple.

I managed to talk Frank into proceeding much more slowly, explaining how rough the ice was and that I was hoping to be able to have children someday. It may have helped that I threatened to void the warranty on his snowmobile, which I had sold him earlier in the year.

As I approached the end of my endurance, Frank spotted a seal and took off after it. I saw nothing until we were within three metres of the poor little guy, who had spotted us and was making for his hole as fast as his flippers would carry him. Somehow, in its panic, the seal seemed to have dived into someone else's hole. He was much too large for his chosen exit and became stuck halfway into the hole.

"Grab him," Frank yelled.

We each grabbed a flipper and heaved with all our might.

It immediately became apparent that the force we used was entirely unnecessary; the seal became airborne, spinning and flailing through the air, landing six metres away from us.

"Don't let him get to the hole!" Frank shouted as he sprinted to the sled to retrieve a weapon of some sort to dispatch the feisty meal.

I stood between the seal and the hole, hoping the seal would not try to attack me to get away. "Hurry, Frank!" I yelled. The seal was now looking me square in the eyes, no doubt sensing my fear.

Then, it happened. The seal came right at me, barking, snarling, and snapping like a dog. With a great lunge, it made for the hole that I was blocking with my legs. Suddenly, our lunch turned on me and decided that I would be on today's menu as he sunk his teeth into my left leg.

As my life flashed before me, Frank appeared out of nowhere and dispatched the seal with a club. He then fell to his knees in the snow and laughed until he cried. Apparently, I was the first white man ever to be attacked by a seal and survive to tell the tale.

I began to peel away layers of clothing, preparing to view the carnage that was once my leg. Miraculously, there was no broken skin. Although the seal's teeth had chewed through all my layers, they had not penetrated my long johns!

Frank butchered the seal and loaded it onto the sled, and my deflated ego and I joined it for the long ride home.

During the week that followed, my bruised and battered body made protest of the abuse I had exposed it to. I was also teased unmercifully. While always eager to explore and learn new things, I had learned that my instinct for survival was much stronger than my search for knowledge. I vowed that there would be no more hunting or camping trips for me. Well, not until the next weekend, anyway, when Frank once again appeared at my door, ready to take me on another excursion.

This time Frank brought me a borrowed snowmobile so that I would not have to ride on the flying komatik of death. He also promised we would stay inland, caribou hunting, where we were in no danger of seal attacks. Reluctantly, I agreed to give it a go and went off in search of my now famous seal-proof long johns.

CAMPING TRIPS AND
CARIBOU KICKS

Frank dropped by and somehow talked me into hunting with him again. I can't believe I agreed to go with him, back to the unforgiving arctic landscape where a carnivorous seal had recently attempted to remove my leg below the knee. But, this time, I would be riding on my own snowmobile, not clutching onto a komatik for dear life. Frank had also promised to stay off the sea ice. In light of the last Arctic Ocean incident, we would be hunting caribou this time. I was also comforted to know that I was sporting the same impermeable, "lucky" long johns that had saved me on the seal-hunting trip. And I had my very own borrowed rifle strapped across my shoulders. I had no idea what to do with it, nor had I ever shot anything before. In any case, I felt a bit better prepared.

We took off with Frank assuming the lead and breaking trail across the tundra. I feel I must point out that the Inuit have two speeds at which they operate their snowmobiles, "full throttle" and "stop for tea." Frank wanted meat and was not in the mood for having tea. He blasted off at full throttle.

I didn't have a lot of experience yet on snowmobiles, and I couldn't believe what I was seeing in front of me, as Frank had become a tiny black dot on the white horizon. I hadn't even put my mitts on yet. I now had to go full throttle myself so I didn't lose sight of him. I figured that if he lost me out there, I'd be taking a long "snow nap." The land looked the same as the sea ice to me. I knew just one thing; I was a white guy in a white world and hadn't a clue how I would survive if I found myself alone on this moonscape. So there I was going full throttle, the wind cutting into my cheeks, trying to keep up with this little black dot on the horizon that I assumed was Frank.

As I drew closer (I was able to catch up only because I was not hauling a komatik loaded with equipment like Frank was), I was able to make out Frank's tail light. Frank motioned that he had spotted signs of the caribou herd. I, on the other hand, was quite pleased with myself for having spotted Frank. We travelled for what seemed like hours, and I felt as if I was going to start bleeding from the kidneys again from all the bumping around. I would never have said anything aloud, but I was starting to wonder if my trusty guide actually knew what he was doing. I hadn't seen a living thing and could swear we were going in circles; absolutely everything was white.

Mercifully, Frank pulled up by the bottom of a hill and upended his komatik to block the wind. He set up his Coleman stove and boiled some snow to make tea. Frank had just about finished his tea by the time I reached him, having fallen behind again because my throttle thumb had frozen. I hopped off my machine for a break.

I was starting to worry about our fuel supply as we seemed to have gone an awfully long way out. I hadn't seen any reserve gasoline on Frank's sled, and I was curious to know how Frank would know when we were halfway through our fuel. But I placed my trust in the guy; he was an Inuk and in his element. I figured he'd be in a lot of trouble if he let a white guy die out here, and he did rescue me from that seal attack a couple of weekends ago. So I just settled in and decided to follow Frank's instructions to the letter, having faith that somehow I would stay alive. I sat down with my mentor and leaned against his komatik. He was choking down a dry frozen hardtack biscuit, chasing it with an object I believed to be a sardine.

I dared not make any assumptions about the food Frank was eating, as the Inuit would eat body parts that I couldn't even recognize or pronounce. But the pilot biscuit was a familiar staple. They were the favourite food of the Inuit people before bread and bannock were introduced by the Scottish Hudson's Bay factors. Pilot biscuits are so hard you can actually drive a nail through them. It is said that if there were ever a nuclear war, two things would survive, pilot biscuits and cockroaches.

Frank offered to share his tea, sardines, and bickies with me. I declined, reminding him that I didn't drink tea. Frank responded, "That's too bad. Tea is what we usually drink up here. I don't have anything else." I helped Frank pack up his utensils and stove, which we then placed in his grub-box.

We both leapt back onto our Ski-Doos and Frank blasted off again at what seemed to be a velocity just slightly slower than the speed of sound. We pulled up by the crest of a drumlin and Frank waved to me to shut off my engine. I think that my machine must have been pretty happy to be turned off at that point. It had been running full throttle for several hours.

Frank motioned to me to take the gun from my shoulder. I lay down flat on the snow and crawled along beside him to the top of the hill. I looked down and there they were: a small gathering of caribou that had broken away from the main herd. There were big caribou, small caribou, caribou with antlers, caribou without antlers, adult caribou, and little baby caribou with spindly legs that looked as if they had just been born and didn't know how to walk. I was thrilled watching the fuzzy little meals walking across the tundra. I felt as if I was starring in a *National Geographic* special.

Frank whispered to me to load my gun.

"With what?" I asked.

"Didn't you take some bullets from the grub-box?" Frank asked in an exasperated tone. "Rifles work better when you put bullets into them. Were you planning to club yourself a caribou today?"

I didn't dignify that comment with a response and began to crawl back to the komatik on my belly as quietly as a city boy could. Returning triumphantly with the ammo, I presented the bullets to Frank. He pointed out that the bullets with which I had returned were for his gun. "Were you planning on shooting today also?" he asked.

"Yes."

"Well, then, you better get back down there and get the bullets in the green box; they will fit your rifle." I dropped to my belly again, which was now growling for a pilot biscuit or sardine. I crawled for what felt like a kilometre across broken glass back to the komatik. Exhausted from all the stealth and cross-country creeping, I soon returned to the site of our ambush. I found Frank having a nap at the top of the hill and snoring so loudly that he had begun to alarm the herd. I didn't want to startle Frank awake for fear he might shoot me. I decided to take a nap myself, from which I was awakened by a rifle shot. Frank was on his knees, rifle raised as he snapped off numerous shots in succession. His face was somewhat pinched; killing was serious business to Frank. He was sweating and the sweat was freezing in his hair.

"We can't shoot more than six. That's all my komatik can carry!" Frank cried out.

"Thanks a lot, Frank, now I have to try to hit a moving target."

Frank frequently hunted for elders and families other than his own because most of the young men were into shooting pool and watching TV, not hunting for food. When we drove back we were planning to drop off the meat to the needy families in the community.

"Frank, this isn't poaching, is it?"

"Go ahead and shoot one. I won't tell anyone," Frank promised. "You can shoot one for me, and I'll take it for my family. I'll bet the community would enjoy knowing that the Bay manager is out here hunting for food in the Inuit way. And that he is generous enough to bring meat back for elders who were unable to hunt."

Well, that sounded good to me.

I took aim with my scope and quickly had an unfortunate individual in my crosshairs. My rifle was much louder than Frank's; it sounded like a cannon going off next to my ear. I saw a caribou fall to the ground, but not the one I had in my sights. A caribou that was foraging two caribou to the left ended up being my hapless victim. Frank shot again and another caribou dropped. That made six.

"Good shooting," Frank commented. "But what's with your eye?"

I hadn't the courage to tell him that it had been a fluke that I had hit anything at all. "My eye?" I hadn't expected the kick from the rifle and the scope had given me a perfectly round shiner.

We walked down the hill to retrieve our snow machines, and proceeded around the hill to claim the spoils of our hunting trip.

Arriving at the scene of our first victim's demise, Frank pulled out a knife and started gutting and skinning it. He certainly had the technique down pat. I couldn't believe how fast he was. He gutted the caribou, skinned it, quartered it, then put the meat back into the skin and tied the legs together. Frank would be considered a skilled surgeon if he were to be observed in any medical school in Canada. My trusted companion then asked if I would please go to his snowmobile and untie the komatik. I was then to use the tow rope to gather the carcasses and bring them to Frank for surgery. He suggested I tie the rope on the caribou's legs and drag them over one at a time.

Frank sat down and, with bloody hands, lit up a cigarette to relax and wait for me to drag the caribou closer. That job sounded good to me, as I didn't know if I had the stomach for butchering one myself. I drove over to the caribou I had shot and was feeling quite proud of myself. Taking the rope in hand, I approached my first "kill" and grabbed the caribou by the back leg. Just as I was about to rope him, the deceitful beast raised his head, looked over his shoulder, and looked me right in the eye. The caribou let fly with a rapid fire of what seemed like twenty or thirty kicks right to my shin. Yes, the same shin the seal had attacked just two weeks before. This time my long underwear didn't help me. He kicked my shins black and blue and then dropped dead.

Frank had seen what had happened, and I wished he hadn't. My guide was rolling on the ground, and he had dropped his cig-arette into the snow. He was hysterical, having once again seen the indigenous wildlife attacking the Bay manager. The smart guy should have been more concerned that his reputation as a guide in the community was going to suffer gravely.

We dragged all the caribou together back to one spot, and Frank taught me how to skin the caribou and quarter it. The trip back was a lot slower as Frank's snowmobile engine laboured under the weight of the meat aboard the komatik. Later, we hop-scotched around the community, dropping off meat to grateful elders who were very happy to have fresh caribou for supper that evening. Frank drove by my house and dropped me off. He lifted my snowmobile as if it weighed nothing, tossed it onto the empty komatik, and drove away. I stood there for a moment, meatless, with a black eye and badly damaged shins, wondering why I always found myself trying to out-Eskimo the Eskimos. I limped into the staff house and removed my torn and bloody long johns, which I no longer thought of as lucky, but which I was then sure carried some sort of curse that causes misfortune.

This was my first catch of the spring after the ice had broken up. Char and trout were a mainstay for the caribou Inuit of Baker Lake, the only Inuit community in the world not situated at the ocean's edge. Seal and walrus meat were unheard of here. (Baker Lake, NU, 1980)

This tiny and most unusual staff house was required to accommodate both the post manager and his trainee. Throw a visiting area manager and accountant into the mix and it would get quite crowded. My clerk slept in the loft and constantly complained of claustrophobia. (Stanley Mission, SK, 1982)

Springtime in Baker Lake. This "No Parking" sign, written in Inuktitut syllabics and English, was almost completely buried under the snow all winter. As the snow melted, the top of the sign revealed where it had been struck by a passing snow-mobile. (Baker Lake, NU, 1980)

This picture shows just about the entire interior of the trading post. We lived in the loft with no power and little heat. We'd open the store when the sun rose and close it when the sun set. That was an economic move, no doubt to save on candles and flashlights. (Ogoki Post, ON, 1979)

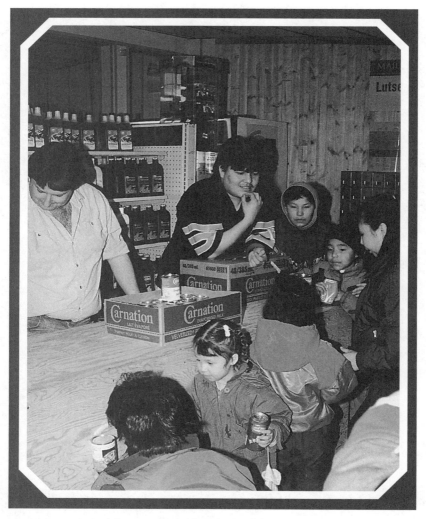

A spring carnival celebration was held in the local store. Here women compete for a prize that goes to the person who can stack soup cans higher than her child. The winner got to take home the soup! Yours truly watches over the festivities. (Lutsel Ké, NWT, 1994)

THE SURLY BONDS
OF EARTH

Bush pilots are the lifeline to everyone who lives or has lived in Canada's north. They are a complex blend of courage, intelligence, and arrogance. They also have a bit of fortune teller in them. I have always felt privileged to have flown with and befriended so many of northern Canada's bush pilots and tundra jumpers. Aviation is probably the most dangerous way to make a living in the north, with the exception of underground mining, of course. More than once I have seen arctic aviators take chances with the weather if saving a life was involved. The brotherhood of the sky flew everything imaginable to everywhere imaginable in

just about every possible condition. Despite all of their prepared-
ness and experience in the world, however, there were accidents.

In the Cree community of Pikangikum, which is near Red
Lake in northwestern Ontario, such an accident occurred just
before Christmas. A leased Air Creebec DC3, flown by Air
Ontario pilots, overshot the tiny community airstrip in an unexpected snow squall. When the pilot banked sharply to avoid the
hilltops, a fuel bladder on board ruptured and caused the ancient
aircraft to crash into the frozen lake below. Two young men lost
their lives that day. Bobbing to the surface was the cargo of toilet paper and Christmas gifts, all surrounded by a pool of fuel oil.

Two lives for a load of toilet paper.

We all keep ourselves going by not dwelling on such calami-
ties. The crash was the furthest thing from my mind when in
August of the following summer I was invited to try a deep-sea
diving rig by the lads from Arctic Divers, who were doing some
underwater welding for the community. I'm talking about one of
those brass, bubble-head helmets you see on TV, screwed into a
dry suit with a hose attached to your head. I almost chickened
out for two reasons. One, the diver guys were laughing way too
hard while trying to stuff me into the suit, while I noticed two
of them were standing on my air hose. Two, someone came up
with the brilliant idea of diving on the plane wreck to see if there
was any salvage down there.

After bolting on the helmet, which made my head feel like it
was in a vise, I was abruptly tossed into the lake. Despite a
twenty-three-kilogram belt of lead weights, I bobbed like a cork.
They reeled me in and put on another weight belt. They all
laughed as I continued to bob about, looking like a fool. I was
reeled in again, attached to a third set of weights, and found
myself shooting to the bottom faster than the *Titanic*. After dis-
lodging myself from the silt on the bottom, I crawled around
the wrecked aircraft looking for salvage. What a mess; those two
pilots hadn't a chance. The aircraft had shattered on impact.
I closed my eyes and imagined the faces of the two young
pilots, whom I had met so many times. I gave the signal to

This DC3 ran into a snow squall on the final approach to Pikangikum's gravel runway. It banked sharply and crashed through the ice on the frozen lake. It was only a few days before Christmas. Such incidents happened entirely too often in the north. Yet there was no shortage of young men who wanted to be bush pilots. (Pikangikum, ON, 1987)

be pulled up to the surface.

As I peeled the diving suit away, I wondered what the young men had thought as the realization of their imminent deaths had overtaken them. I tried to remember the face of every pilot I had ever met in the north and could not. They deserve better than that, I thought.

I promised myself that day to share their stories with all who would listen, and to always be thankful to the flying men and women of the Canadian north.

THE FLIGHT OF CHEESE
CHARTER ONE

I suppose it makes a lot of sense to have a backup plan when flying in the Arctic, such as having two engines rather than one. An airline trying to make a go of it with only one aircraft would be out of business faster than you could say "Punch Dickens."

Back in the late seventies, when I was based in Baker Lake, we were serviced by a small airline called Lamb Air. They were running two DC3s out of Winnipeg via Churchill, Manitoba. The fleet of two consisted of one aircraft that had heat, and another, affectionately known as the "old one," that did not. Apparently, the "old one" was constructed in 1945 rather than in 1946, thus making it substandard.

I was somewhat alarmed when I first saw these aircraft. I knew I had seen them somewhere previously, and it came to me later that I had seen several Second World War films in which paratroopers were hurling themselves out the doors of these old girls. Now here they were in Baker Lake, still in use and probably no longer under warranty. They looked like torpedoes with wings stuck on them. For added effect, some genius had glued a little wheel on the tail, which was very similar to the bockity wheels you usually end up getting on your shopping cart when you are out buying groceries.

Strangely, however, they seemed to get the job done, and I eventually got used to seeing them overhead and underfoot, and became less worried about them. Those aircraft were our lifeline and became a reality in my daily life.

I found that after about six months in Baker Lake as the grocery manager, I needed a change of vocation. It was time to hire somebody new from southern Canada and bring him up. I was to train that person to be my successor before I would be able to step aside and move into the fascinating world of hardware and socks.

My grocery successor arrived one day on the hot DC3, which popped out of the clouds and limped to the airstrip on one engine. A very tall, very sweaty fellow got off the plane. He had the remains of airsickness on his chin. He offered me his hand, which I declined, as I noticed similar remains on his hands as well. Lanky Pete had arrived.

He was a blond fellow from Belleville, Ontario, just west of the centre of Pete's universe. Pete was a bit of a cowboy. There wasn't much you could tell him when trying to train him. It seemed as though he knew everything already and didn't listen to much of what I was telling him. He had an annoying habit of talking overtop of me: "Ya, ya, ya. I know, I know, I know."

In the late seventies, the telephone systems of the Arctic consisted of very primitive surplus equipment from the south, circa 1928. We had to dial out and get a sequence operator in

Montreal, and keep dialling out to get a sequence operator in Montreal who could speak English. When you finally hit one, you would ask her to stay on the line so that you could make a series of phone orders in sequence. We would sit down with our grocery orders for the week, and one by one the operator would dial for us. We would place our orders verbally, and the operator would stay on the line until we had finished. As you can imagine, not having things written down could create some problems. One had to be very clear and specific at all times. I tried to emphasize this to the Lanky One, and to make sure he asked the supplier to repeat everything back to him. Pete found this rather amusing and did not take me seriously. For example, if you were ordering one hundred pounds of hamburger in one-pound packages, you had to be very specific about the one-pound packages or you would end up with a cow on your doorstep. Lanky Pete went to the manager one day and decided that he had received enough training and that he was fully prepared to revolutionize the industry. In turn, I immersed myself in the world of screwdrivers, snowmobile parts, and chainsaws. I never could figure out why they had chainsaws in the Arctic because there were no trees—but hey, if they sold, we carried them.

Lanky Pete set about his business on behalf of The Honourable Company and soon found himself ordering cheese. I thought I had overheard him ordering incorrectly and asked him to pause for a moment so I might speak with him. With a sweep of his hand, he waved me off.

The following week, we received a panicked phone call from someone at the airport. He said that there was an unscheduled flight coming in on Lamb Air. Some sort of garbled mayday had been heard. Apparently, there was a crisis that involved our groceries. The crew would have to unload hurriedly, turn around, and get back to Churchill as quickly as possible. Pete and I sprinted to the truck and took off for the airstrip. We were scanning the sky and waiting for the DC3 to appear. I noticed that the cockpit windows were cracked open and that the aircraft took a steep angle into the strip as if it were making an emergency landing. Then something quite unusual occurred.

Usually after the aircraft taxied in, the crew would wait until the propellers stopped turning before they opened the door. On this particular flight, the door fell open on the tail of the aircraft while the aircraft and propellers were still in motion. Out of the fuselage spilled a tangle of arms, legs, and other assorted body parts. We could see that there was some problem on board. We thought perhaps some exhaust fumes were leaking in or a fuel problem had caused the crew to gag and gasp for air. All of them looked quite ill. When we saw the pilots bailing out, we knew that we had a serious incident on our hands. I was looking at the paint on the aircraft, which indicated to me that it was the hot DC3, not the "old one."

The plane had been loaded to capacity with groceries—or so said the manifest. We went to assist the crew, who were now crawling across the tarmac on their hands and knees. They all had tears in their eyes. We had to ask the pilot why the flight crew—who usually hung around to help us unload the aircraft—had all crawled past us and into the air terminal. As we began unloading the groceries without any help, it quickly became apparent what the problem was. As we stuck our heads in the door, the stench of cheese was almost too much to bear. We examined the freight and noted that all there was on the aircraft was cheese. The aircraft was loaded to capacity with ten-pound blocks of every kind of cheese you could possibly imagine.

It seems that Lanky Pete, while ordering the previous week, had neglected to ask for smaller wedges of plastic-wrapped cheese like the ones you see in the grocery store. He had in fact ordered by the case lot, each case containing two ten-pound blocks of cheese.

The hot aircraft had made the five-hour flight from Churchill with the cabin temperature in excess of thirty degrees Celsius. The cheese had turned into vapour and had pretty near exterminated the crew during the flight. We left the cheese on the aircraft and jumped into the truck to drive as quickly as we could back to the store to summon the manager, Doug. Pete explained

I am no longer the grocery manager and I find myself thrown into the world of men's socks and underwear. Notice my attire matches the garments hanging on the racks. There was nowhere else to shop! That is why all HBC personnel could easily be picked out of any crowd. (Baker Lake, NU, 1980)

to him that "someone" had made some sort of mistake, that the grocery charter sitting at the airport was obviously someone else's cheese charter. Doug thought we were joking at first, but when he saw how serious we were and caught a whiff of our clothing, he knew we were not kidding.

He sprinted to the truck and tore off for the airport on his own, leaving us behind to prepare for unemployment. He was back within a few minutes, looking a little green around the gills. He told us not to move and to wait for him right there; he had to make a phone call. Doug made a couple of phone calls and came back with some bad news. The aircraft was fuelled to fly into Baker Lake fully loaded; however, it was not carrying enough fuel to fly back with the same weight on board. The cheese had to be removed.

We went back to the airport and set about loading the truck with cheese. It took us two trips to get all the cheese back to the warehouse behind the store. Doug chose to move the cheese into an unheated warehouse and wisely so.

We had a short meeting after we had done a cheese inventory and set about trying to figure a way out of this mess-au-gratin. I suggested a cheese festival. That idea was quickly thrown out; we all agreed that the company had messed up the Inuit culture enough already.

We tried to return the cheese, but the manufacturer didn't feel responsible for having misjudged the cheese needs of the Inuit of the Canadian Arctic. They had been more than happy to send us a planeload of cheese but proved reluctant to repossess it. We ended up having a cheese sale, and actually got out a hot plate, a loaf of bread, and a frying pan and started making grilled cheese sandwiches in the store, hoping the smell would entice people to purchase cheese.

Pete, who was no longer on speaking terms with the manager or me, was in the back with a chainsaw taking chunks of cheese off the huge blocks and wrapping them for our customers. At first we did very well; when something is the right price people get excited about it. However, there is a theory that involves markets and saturation that is based on the population of your community, the availability of the product, and need. In this case the availability of product far exceeded the need. The market became saturated when we had moved about two hundred pounds of cheese.

The over-cheesed Inuit began to request refunds. Let me point out here that the R-word does not exist in the HBC dictionary. We offered to give them double their cheese back as a reward and an apology for their difficulties with our quality product. The quality of cheese that we provided to make amends was of the same poor quality as the cheese that was being returned in the first place. Reluctant to allow the cheese crisis to create bad faith with our customers, we ended up leaving the cheese frozen in the warehouse, hoping we could figure out what to do with it before spring. I didn't mind that plan as I had already received my transfer papers and would be leaving Baker Lake before spring arrived. I had received the call that I was to be made manager of my own post.

I left Lanky Pete behind with his warehouse full of cheese and found myself sitting on a DC3, getting heatstroke as I belted myself in. I did my best to look as innocent as possible as I watched the other passengers sniffing the air, looking around, and trying to figure out which dirty rotter had "cut the cheese" on that flight.

THE CHICKEN WING
BANDITS

When I was working in Baker Lake in the 1980s, a wire basket stretcher called a Stokes stretcher was a common sight. In the north, when a medivac was necessary, these stretchers were used to carry bundled patients onto planes, which then set out for Yellowknife, Churchill, Montreal, or the closest place with a hospital. If you were on land when you were hurt, you would be wrapped in a hypothermia suit before being placed on the stretcher. This is because by the time you arrived at the nursing station, you were likely suffering not only from your injuries or illness but from hypothermia as well. A hypothermia suit looks like a sleeping bag from the outside, but the inside is lined with a special foil that conserves body heat for many hours. Sometimes the hypothermia suit in Baker Lake was used to conserve heat from other items as well.

In the north in the 1980s, we did not have the luxury of fast food. However, many of the non-indigenous persons who lived in northern communities occasionally had cravings for Chinese food, pizza (known as a "grease wheel"), Kentucky Fried Chicken, or for McDonald's Big Macs (known as "gut grenades"). Fortunately, we were sometimes able to use our "in" to get our hands on some fast food. Whenever a nurse accompanied a stretcher and patient in a hypothermia suit out of Baker Lake to Winnipeg, she would contact the network of non-indigenous persons in the community and a quick collection would take place, followed by an order for a fast food feast of some description. The nurse would place the fast food in the hypothermia bag in Winnipeg and zip it up for the return trip. It would then be unzipped, revealing piping hot pizza, chicken, or McDonald's cuisine that would be served straight out of the suit and thoroughly enjoyed by the numerous displaced urbanites.

On one such occasion, a medivac took place in the wee hours of the morning. The RCMP corporal was the only member of the fast food network who was awake, so he placed and financed an order on our collective behalf. Corporal Ed gave the nurses a large amount of money and asked them if they would order a feast of Kentucky Fried Chicken with all of the trimmings. The nurses were very excited and gladly took his money to Winnipeg, where they first went about their non-chicken business with the patient involved. Then they went to the nearest Kentucky Fried Chicken restaurant and loaded a taxi with chicken and all the fixings. At the airport, the greasy repast was loaded into the hypothermia suit, zipped up, and put back on the plane for the trip home.

The next day, late on Saturday morning, Corporal Ed called me and another Hudson's Bay trainee named Chris to meet the plane. He asked us to go to the airport and assist the nurses coming off the plane because he was tied up with somebody he had arrested earlier in the day. He was questioning, fingerprinting, and photographing a young man who had taken the priest's snowmobile for a joyride. We were to meet the nurses, rescue the fast food, and rush it back to the RCMP staff house, where Ed's wife would lay out the feast. The fast food network would then hit the phones and call everybody in for the big feast.

We met the nurses at the aircraft and unloaded the stretcher. Unzipping the hypothermia suit, we took all of the chicken and other fixings and put them on the front seat and the floor of the truck. Zipping the suit back up, the nurses took the stretcher back to the nursing station. They told us they would drop over to the RCMP officer's house within the hour.

Chris and I started driving back toward the village. When we got to the fork in the road, the proverbial fork in the road, we should have taken the path to the left and gone into town. The right thing would have been to bring the chicken directly to Ed's house. However, we sat together at the fork and seemed to have the same idea at the same time. Chris and I looked at one another and knew we could no longer wait to do something about the heavenly aroma filling the cab of the truck. "Let's take the other road and drive out to the dump. No one will see us there and we can have a look in the boxes and see what Officer Ed ordered," I said. I noticed Chris was now drooling on his shirt, and I suspect I was as well.

The aroma of fried chicken was too much to bear. We had gone without at this Arctic outpost for much too long. Chris and I drove over to the dump and parked ourselves behind a mountainous cluster of old rusted-out vehicles. Feeling safe and knowing that we hadn't been noticed by anyone, we opened a box. In the box were four buckets of chicken. There were four more buckets of chicken in another box. The rest of the boxes contained salads, french fries, gravy, and other fixings.

The Colonel had been very kind to us. I looked at Chris and said, "You know, I love chicken wings and it's been at least two years since I had one. Why don't we just grab a piece of chicken each? We'll try it out. Who's going to notice a couple of missing pieces? We could have a mini-feast right here and then quickly get back to town while it is still hot." Chris pointed out that he was also a chicken wing fanatic. Without any further discussion, we each grabbed one of the plump little beauties and scarfed them, throwing the bones out the window to the delight of the orbiting dump gulls above.

However, we found that chicken wings are like potato chips—you can't just eat one. We looked at one another and agreed to take one more each, assuring ourselves that no one would notice. Needless to say, fifteen minutes later we were both stuffed to the gills, and there wasn't a wing left in any of the buckets. We looked at each other and hung our heads in shame. We had greasy fingers and guilty looks on our faces and figured we had better get back while the rest of the chicken was still hot.

Darting back to the community, we stopped at the RCMP officer's house. His wife was waiting at the front window and was quite angry that we had taken so long on the short trip from the airstrip. She scolded us as we carried the boxes in and threatened that if the chicken were cold she would borrow her husband's service revolver and kneecap the pair of us.

We were in a lot of trouble.

After unloading all the chicken fixings, we noticed that people had already started to arrive. They were appearing on snowmobiles, three-wheel motorcycles, trucks, cars, and dogsleds, descending on the staff house. Ed's wife pointed out that the corporal was still busy at the detachment but would be back momentarily. She asked that we all get comfortable while she set up the buffet. In the end, it was a beautiful thing to behold. The people who had arrived were circling the table just as the gulls had circled above us at the dump.

Shortly, I heard some keys jingling in the door. In walked a man who was so large he had to dip his head so he wouldn't bang it on the door frame on the way in. It was Corporal Ed, who looked like a refrigerator with striped pants. Ed was one of the biggest men I have ever seen. Doors were definitely not designed for him; his shoulders touched both sides of the frame as he entered. He looked hungry and frustrated from a long day at the detachment.

He came in and greeted everyone and pointed out that there would be no collection required today as it was his treat. Ed was a generous man. But Ed had one request: he asked that no one eat any of the chicken wings. Apparently, he loved chicken wings and hadn't had them in many months. Everything else on the table was fair game.

Chris looked and me, and I was already looking back at him. We were hoping no one would notice our greasy faces, lips, and fingers. We slowly inched our way out of the far corner of the room and from beneath the officer's immense shadow. We stealthily tiptoed towards the door. Everybody dug in like a pack of half-starved ravens tearing into a garbage bag. Ed was dumping one bucket after another, seeking out his wings. After going through all eight buckets, he was now cursing at the top of his lungs at the "Kentucky Fried Bastards" who dared to deprive him of chicken wings after all the money he had spent on this feast.

Ed had managed to get through a long and terrible day in anticipation of having more than his fill of chicken wings. He was so upset that he picked up the phone and called information for the number of the Kentucky Fried Chicken in Winnipeg that was near the airport. The manager of the restaurant received a blast that I don't think he will ever forget for not including any wings. The manager was quite upset as well, and he pointed out that he had, in fact, packed the order himself and that there were at least four wings in each of the buckets. He couldn't possibly offer any explanation for why they weren't there after the plane trip. The manager apologized while still recovering from the abuse he had just endured. Ed slammed down the receiver. Infuriated, the wingless RCMP officer started breathing very heavily. He looked a lot like a muskox ready to charge.

Everyone looked at the nurses, who shrugged, and then looked at us. We must have looked a little greasy or chickenish or something. There was something about the way we looked that instantly gave away our crime. We made for the door as quickly as we could, two steps across the room. In a split second, the corporal had us both by the scruff of our necks, our feet no longer touching the floor. We were hustled out the door without time to put on our jackets or boots. It was thirty below outside, but Ed hardly noticed as he dragged us to the RCMP detachment. Throwing us through the door, he opened the cell, pushed us both in, then slammed the door and locked it.

On his way out the door, he motioned for the janitor, who was quietly mopping the floor. The janitor was an older Inuit man with whom he exchanged words in Inuktitut. I have no idea what was said because I had not yet learned the local dialect. Ed left and went back to the big feast. We thought that he was upset and that in a couple of minutes he would cool off and come back to let us out.

Two hours later, we were still sitting in the cell, begging the janitor, who apparently did not speak any English, to hand us the telephone as the cord was long enough to reach the cell. He kept shrugging to indicate that he did not know what we were saying to him. I tried to gesture and pantomime our message to him, that this was all a joke and would he hand me the keys to the cell.

He did not show any indication that he understood what I was trying to say to him. The janitor then vanished for about an hour and a half. We waited impatiently to be released. Both of us felt remorse for the unforgivable chicken crime that we had committed. We had humiliated ourselves in front of the entire non-indigenous community of Baker Lake.

After we had been in the cell for five hours, the janitor came back to finish his duties. The smell of chicken accompanied him. We once again attempted to pantomime a plea, this time for him to call the Bay manager. We hoped that the manager could talk the RCMP officer into letting us out based on time served. The janitor simply shrugged. A few minutes later, Corporal Ed walked in. He'd had the big feast and his nap and had come by to see how his prisoners were doing. We both apologized profusely and offered to pay for the chicken we had eaten. Corporal Ed looked at us with scorn and didn't say a word. He opened the door, threw our coats and boots at us, and told us to get out; he never wanted to see us again.

Ed was fingering his holster in an intimidating manner. Chris didn't wait around to find out what would happen next; he took off. I was on his heels, preparing to hear the crack of a gunshot and feel the life ebbing from my body. I distinctly remember hearing the elderly Inuit man behind us, laughing and talking to the RCMP officer in clear English. "So those are the two little buggers that stole all of your chicken wings." I heard them both roaring with laughter as we headed down the road past the RCMP staff house, where the banquet had long since ended. We went back to our staff house, where we hung our heads in shame and prepared to be outcasts in our tiny community. "People seem to take their chicken very seriously up here," I thought.

I found myself removed from the fast food network for the rest of the winter. I was disappointed in myself for getting into that situation. But for every problem, there is a solution; I soon made the acquaintance of a young man who was bootlegging ten-buck Big Macs, which took care of my cravings for fast food.

THE TWO
MATRIARCHS

The Hudson's Bay Company enjoyed a monopoly in northern Canada for more than three hundred years. In its long life, it had developed retail into a science wherein nothing was ever left to chance. Each post had stockbook selections that were honed by many generations of factors. They recorded credit histories on families that began with great-grandparents and moved on to the grandparents and parents in the communities. We all knew which families were good credit risks and which ones displayed similar purchasing ethics and characteristics. The HBC had gathered so much economic and cultural intelligence over the years that easily maintained control over the local economies.

The first serious challenge to the Bay's economic dominance in the north came from a most unlikely source: Japan. The arrival of the resupply barge that year in late August revealed the encroachment of a new Yamaha snowmobile dealership; no one failed to notice the mountain of Yamaha crates stacked as deck freight. Since the invention of the snowmobile, the Hudson's Bay Company had enjoyed an exclusive in the north, with no serious challengers. It was the sole supplier of sleds and lucrative snow-mobile parts. But this was Baker Lake, the only community of inland Inuit on the planet.

Unlike their Inuit cousins farther north, the people living around Baker Lake did not have access to seal and whale meat. They didn't go out to sea for food, but stayed on the enormous expanse of land that surrounded Baker Lake. They lived on a freshwater lake and were known as the people of the caribou. Being land-based hunters, they sure loved their snowmobiles. The bigger and more powerful, the better, which makes sense since the tundra around Baker Lake was the roughest place on the planet. Hummocks, rock, and other glacial features were most disagreeable with current snowmobile technology. Bombardier would have cringed to see the beating its machines were taking in the Arctic. Snowmobiles carried the people's hunters all over that rough terrain; they were indispensable to the local economy and a great seller at the Bay.

Every fall, the barge came in to restock all the grocery supply needs for the entire community for a year. The last thing unloaded was the deck freight, which usually consisted of numerous crates of building materials or semi-assembled crated snowmobiles. You would think that the HBC would be able to land enough machinery to satisfy the needs of such a tiny community. But we always seemed to come up short. I imagine that situation was what created the vacuum that allowed Yamaha to come north.

Yamaha's machines were built differently than Ski-Doos. The big advantage to them was that their retail price was so low.

Yamaha's parent company in Tokyo paid the freight for Yamaha equipment to anywhere in North America. As a result, a Yamaha snowmobile would sell for the same price whether you were in Toronto or Tuktoyaktuk. This was not the case for our Canadian-made machines. We had to pay a buck-a-pound freight charge to get them up there, and we passed that cost along to our customers. As a result, Yamaha anticipated a huge demand in the Arctic market; they shipped so many units that year that I am sure they outnumbered the caribou herd of the region. There was panic at the Hudson Bay House in Winnipeg that shook it to its three-hundred-year-old roots. The costly machines we brought up north became more and more sophisticated every year—more expensive and much more difficult to repair.

I don't know who designed the Yamaha snowmobiles, but I suspect it was the same individual who designed those little plastic red poppies that we all pin to our lapels for Remembrance Day. As I recall, the poppies usually go on sale on 1 November, and everyone ends up buying two or three every day for the following eleven days. They seem to be designed to go flying off at the slightest breeze or jostle. As a result, the sidewalks of any Canadian city in early November resemble Flanders Fields on a spring day.

At any rate, Yamaha must have hired this guy because their machines displayed a similar quality: parts would go flying off at the most inopportune moments, never to be found again. People would end up back at the dealer buying a part no bigger than your thumb for two hundred dollars. It was a good scam, and we were resentful: parts and machines had been our gig for so many years.

Even though the parts were inclined to fly away, the Yamaha machines were beautiful when they were assembled, very sporty-looking and very racy compared to the Bombardier creations, which were old workhorses and pretty damn ugly to boot. However, Ski-Doos had been in the north since the advent of the snowmobile. Even though we were nervous about the new Yamaha dealership, we still thought we would be okay because people like to stick with what they know and are not always eager to explore new things. We were very wrong.

We ended up overstocked with many Ski-Doos at the end of that year's snowmobile season. Yamaha sold out every unit it had, appealing to every part of Baker Lake's small market.

The new dealer had brought in two deluxe Lady Machines, which were tiny, easy to start, and suitable for an elder or lady. This was smart, as the machines that had previously populated the community were huge, powerful, and very cranky to start in cold weather. The Lady Machines were made from aluminum rather than steel and were only suitable for use in town; they would be no match for the tundra.

There were several matriarchs in Baker Lake, and they were perpetually in competition to display who had the most beautiful kamiks or parka, or who had been given the best gift, displaying the depth of love and respect from her family. The gifts also seemed to display how successful a family was and how the family held influential and lofty positions within the community. It was only a matter of time before one of the families purchased a hot new vehicle for one of these elderly women.

Mary Louise, matriarch of the wealthiest family in Baker Lake, received the very first Lady Machine as a gift from her extended family. It was a shiny blue sled and very sporty-looking. The morning she received it, Mary drove the machine from one end of the town to the other, up and down the main street over and over again. I was starting to wonder what kind of gasoline economy she was getting, as she did not stop for the entire morning. In fact, she did not stop cruising until she was sure that everyone in the village had seen what a wonderful new machine her family had bought for her. She was grinning from ear to ear despite the absence of teeth.

Of course, the second largest family in the community saw what was going on and went directly to the dealer to get the other machine for their grandma. Before long, Bessie was riding around on her brand new gleaming snowmobile, as proud as an arctic peacock. Here we were, many miles above the Arctic

My first snowmobile! It was a used 1977 Ski-Doo Olympic, the last of the steel-bodied sleds, before aluminum ones took their place. It cost me four hundred bucks to purchase and five hundred to fix it. In the Arctic, snowmobiles are like cars. You do not want to find yourself a pedestrian at forty below. (Baker Lake, NU, 1980)

Circle, and people were still trying to "keep up with the Joneses"; I guess some things transcend all cultures and geography.

Bessie's machine was bright red and had so much chrome on it you could hardly see her. She resembled a star lost in the aurora borealis. The aged ex-pedestrian followed Mary's lead and drove around and around on the peacock circuit. She made sure she stopped in front of the Bay store, in front of the church, the post office, and the community hall. It was inevitable that eventually the two matriarchs would meet up somewhere.

Early the next day, both ladies came out to cruise around the community, just in case anyone had missed them the previous

127

day. It was almost as if neither matriarch was aware that she was not the only one with such an extravagant mode of transportation. It was just before sunset, and we are talking spring here, so the sun was just beginning to climb back into the sky. Both women had decided on one more pass down the main drag past the Co-op Hotel. They were heading directly towards one another on the same trail beside the road. Both ladies were so shocked to see the other riding such a lovely new machine that they neglected to hit the brakes.

The two elders hit head on, locking their skis. The collision sent both of them flying off headfirst into the soft snow at the side of the road. Thier machines were utterly destroyed. The accident scene resembled a Russian satellite that had crashed to Earth: there were hundreds and hundreds of unidentifiable little Yamaha pieces all over the place. Both ladies were sitting—lips quivering —in the snow, totally puzzled about how this could have happened.

The next season our snowmobile sales picked up again and we found a supplier who provided us with generic snowmobile parts that fit both Ski-Doo and Yamaha machines. That fall I saw Bessie walking down the main street past Mary's house with a huge boombox, which was bigger than she was, on her shoulder, blasting Johnny Cash tunes at full volume.

HARD TIMES AT THE SUGAR SHACK

Prior to barge time at Baker Lake, which was usually around August or early September, all the Bay warehouses had to be cleaned up from the previous year's resupply. In that community, the Hudson's Bay store was quite small in comparison to the massive warehouses required to store all the grocery needs for the entire community for a year. There were specific warehouses for items that were extremely big sellers. One example of a commodity-specific warehouse was the sugar shack. It was stacked wall to wall and floor to ceiling with bales of sugar. There was also a Carnation milk shack, a pop shack, and a maze of other heated and unheated warehouses that had their various uses. The community seemed to be accustomed to drinking one-year-old pop, even though after a year in storage, soft drinks would begin to eat through the cans, once even flooding the warehouse floor.

Doug, the manager of the store at Baker Lake, had become something of a grouch since I had come to the outpost. It seemed he had been promised a transfer to head office, but his move had been put on hold. He had become testy as a result, especially right before the resupply barge came in. He thought he would already have cleared out before having to land yet another barge of groceries. Keep in mind the volume of the supplies required to carry a community for an entire year and you may understand his pique.

We worked around the clock for three days unloading the barge. We also pumped a year's worth of fuel from the barge into the holding tanks. The barge would then make a mad dash for open water before freeze-up. And just when we thought the work was all done, we had to do an inventory and get everything squared away in the warehouses before winter set in.

Doug had resigned himself to preparing the warehouses to receive the following year's freight. Barge time that year must have seemed like the appropriate time for him to settle old scores. I must have committed some sin of which I have no memory, as Doug singled me out to prepare the dreaded sugar shack.

"John," he said, "I want you to get the remaining sugar and carry it back to the farthest warehouse, right to the end of the heated warehouse run."

We are talking about thirty-seven-kilogram bales here, and we didn't have anything with wheels on it to make the job easier. And, if we did, it would be unusable. Our warehouse system consisted of old Bay stores and pieces of old buildings that had been nailed together. Everything was connected by stairs, ramps, or tunnels, none of which were level. Each warehouse looked as if someone had taken a chainsaw, cut a hole in the wall, and glued it to the building. I asked if it would be possible to hire some people to move the sugar down the tunnels by chain gang.

For some reason, Doug always seemed to take offence to any suggestion that required brains over brawn. He ignored my suggestion and assigned me the task of consolidating and removing all the leftover sugar from the previous year to make way for the crew to come in and clean the warehouse. I couldn't believe he expected me to get all of the work done before the barge was due to arrive, two days from then. There were hundreds and hundreds of bales of sugar stacked to the ceiling. The Inuit sure loved their sugar.

I recall my shock the first time I saw an Inuit person making tea. He shovelled eight spoons of sugar into his mug while smiling at me through black and broken teeth. After he stirred the soupy mess that was once a mug of tea, he licked off the goopy spoon and downed it. What was left was an inch of brown sludge, which he devoured with gusto.

It would be the notorious Inuit sweet tooth that would help me to empty the sugar shack.

I went home that night very discouraged, knowing I was there to pay my dues in order to rise through the ranks of the Honourable Company. I was, however, determined to think of a better way to prepare the sugar shack for the resupply barge. I invited a couple of my Inuit co-workers, James and Alex, for a brainstorm on my dilemma. I was hoping that they would help me in my scheme to lessen my workload.

I had visited them on many occasions when I was new to the community, and recalled asking the guys why nobody had phones in their houses. I had been to other communities, smaller than Baker Lake, where the people had phones. For example, in northern Ontario I had done a relief job at a post called Cat Lake. There was an old log store that had to be wrapped with Saran Wrap every winter so the snow wouldn't run through the building. In the tiny community, there was a rather slim directory containing ten phone numbers. The chief had a phone in his office that, of course, was number 1; there was one in the Bay, one in the post office, and God only knows where the rest of them

Each arctic post had immense warehouses where we stored all of the community's needs for an entire year. As barge time approached each fall, the warehouses had to be cleared and cleaned to receive the new stock. Run out of anything and there was hell to pay! (Baker Lake, NU, 1980)

were. The fascinating thing was that in order to phone somebody, you just had to dial one number. I just couldn't believe how many times my phone rang and it was a wrong number.

James had informed me that in the Baker Lake community, phones were not popular because CB radios were all the rage. Families and groups of friends had their own channels. The channels were divided strategically amongst the community. It was considered bad form to intrude on someone else's frequency. The CBs gave me a really good idea.

I asked James and Alex what would happen if the Bay were to run out of sugar before the barge came in.

"Oh, that would be really bad!" Alex said.

James was shaking his head in agreement. Both thought that if such a catastrophe were to occur, somebody might try to kill us. You just don't run out of sugar in the Arctic and live to tell the tale. That explained why the warehouse was still full of sugar with the barge scheduled to arrive in only a few days. I asked James and Alex if they would consider doing a little job for me for ten bucks.

James and Alex were both great pranksters and they agreed to my plan. I wrote a little script for each of them and sent them home with a small schedule.

Every quarter-hour, starting at channel one, my contract jokesters were to dial onto a channel and read their scripts until they had been on all twenty-three channels. The scripts read as follows:

"James, I'm calling James. Are you out there, James?"

"I read you, Alex. What can I do for you?"

"Did you have a good day at work today at the Bay?"

"Yes, I did, but have you heard the news?"

"No, I didn't!"

"We are almost out of sugar, just a few bags left. The manager is very upset. He thinks somebody is going to try and kill him when we run out of sugar!"

"There is going to be big trouble!"

"Did you bring home some sugar today, James?"

"I did."

"Me too. I got all the sugar I could pay for. I don't have any sugar money left! My family is not going to run out of sugar."

"Neither is mine!"

The next morning, the manager was scratching his head as he went to open the front doors. The people from the community had formed an unruly line that extended the entire length of the store. Nobody let on that they had been eavesdropping on someone else's conversation. But if there actually was a sugar crisis, the people in the line were determined not to be affected. They decided to nonchalantly grab a supply of sugar that would keep

When the supply barge arrived, the entire community came to a halt. Everyone participated in unloading the community's supplies. Beneath the deck of each barge, massive tanks hauled in the fuel needs of the community for the coming year. Later on, communities became less interested in the ceremonial aspect of the barge's arrival and more interested in earning wages for their efforts unloading. (Baker Lake, NU, 1980)

them until barge time, just to be safe.

We spent the rest of the morning hauling sugar from the warehouse the short distance to the store. The sugar and other heavy items are routinely kept in the warehouses closest to the store because they are difficult to move. By the end of the day, we had rung up a great day's sales, and there was not a bag of sugar left to be had. People who arrived late discovered that the rumour had been true! The Bay was out of sugar.

JESSE AND THE
FISHING JIG

When I first arrived in the Arctic, it was in the dead of winter. I promptly began waiting for spring to arrive because I had heard that the days grew long and got a lot warmer. Of course, the Inuit were out and about regardless of the weather or the cold; they seemed to be in harmony with their environment. I was dying to get out and meet the people of Baker Lake and learn more about their culture.

One day I awoke early and glanced out my window overlooking the harbour of Baker Lake, around which the community had grown. To my surprise, it appeared that half of the community was out on the ice. It was very early in the morning so I was puzzled about what was going on. I quickly dressed and went down to the harbour. I noticed that the ice had been bored through with numerous holes and everyone, young or old, was fishing. What seemed to be a community event had the atmosphere of a spring carnival.

The Inuit were everywhere, sitting, standing, perched on snowmobiles; children were playing, running; elders were smoking and telling stories. Despite all the activity, everybody had a line and was fishing. Some older people who recognized me from the Bay flagged me over and gestured to me to throw in a fishing line for myself.

I told them I loved to fish and they provided me with a caribou antler fishing rig with fishing twine wrapped around it and a huge red devil spoon with a little piece of pork dangling from the barbed tips. They pointed me towards a hole of my own, located beside an old lady named Jesse Oonaark, who was fishing there with a couple of her grandchildren. I was amazed to see the size of the fish people were pulling out of the holes. It was a wonder that the holes were big enough at all, as some of the children were walking around displaying fish that were bigger than they were. The fish were incredibly big in comparison to the ones I had pulled from Grenadier Pond in High Park, downtown Toronto.

I had been ice fishing before and thought that I was quite knowledgeable about the activity. I dipped my hook down into the hole and squatted there, jigging and enjoying the spring sun warming my face. I watched the children play and listened to the joy and laughter that surrounded me. I started to feel that perhaps I could be a part of this community too.

The hours went by, and everybody was pulling fish after fish from their holes. Some folks whipped out the family ulu (a knife shaped like a half moon) and started eating the fish raw. I, on the other hand, was catching nothing.

Seeing that I was having bad luck, Jesse wandered over and loudly said something to me in Inuktitut that I didn't understand.

Everyone standing within earshot began laughing. I also laughed at the joke, even though I did not get it and surmised that it no doubt involved sushi and was probably on me. I had assumed that they were laughing at the fact that I had been there for so many hours and had caught nothing.

Jesse pulled in my line and gave me a poke in the ribs. Actually it was more like a dig in the ribs that almost knocked the breath out of me. She seized the fishing antler from my frozen little hands and wound the fishing line back onto the antler with two or three strokes. Jessie once again reprimanded me in Inuktitut and then started laughing so hard that she began to cry. Everyone broke into gales of laughter, and I'm sure my frozen face turned beet red. Why would they be laughing at me? Of all the things that went on up here, this was the one activity that I knew something about.

In northern Ontario, in the middle of winter, the ice is at its thickest on the lakes. Ontario ice fishermen have to cut through two or three feet of ice in order to fish. I have actually driven vehicles on Ontario lakes with no fear of breaking through. We would drop in three or four feet of line and start pulling in the ravenous trout.

The problem here was that I didn't realize that the ice of Baker Lake was six to eight feet thick. I had let out about four feet of line and had been fishing within the confines of my fishing hole for many hours. To the joy and delight of all of my Inuit neighbours, in this one ice fishing lesson they had taught me how little I knew of their land, Nunavut, and their ways.

SAM'S JOHN HENRY

The Hudson's Bay Company took the fur business very seriously, as did the Inuit trappers and hunters who traded furs with it. As we watched the fur trade collapse around us in the 1980s, we wondered what would become of the families of trappers who had always been loyal to the Bay. There were other fur buyers on the scene at the time, but the HBC still seemed to get the lion's share of the trade.

Being from the last generation of fur traders was not an honour for me. Fur trading had been the best part of the job, but slowly we were being trained to be shopkeepers rather than fur traders. I was disappointed in the change within my vocation. I had felt that being in the Arctic, I was on the last frontier on

138

Earth, the last place where one could live apart from the trappings of western civilization.

Since I was interested in the trade, I always got to know the trappers by name and by reputation. In my first year with the company, I had been bounced from northern Ontario to northern Saskatchewan, and then to the Northwest Territories. All of the transferring was necessary for me to gain experience with as many species of fur-bearing animals as possible. The Cree and Ojibwa peoples of northern Ontario acquainted me with beaver, black bear, mink, martin, ermine, fisher, lynx, and a plethora of foxes. (I also got to know the skunk in northern Ontario, but that's another story.) The Cree and Chipeweyan peoples of Saskatchewan offered coyote, wolf, beaver, otter, muskrat, and the plentiful and annoying red squirrel. In my new Arctic home, I discovered the wolverine, seals of many types, polar bear, and the jewel of the north, the white Arctic fox. In every outpost, I found that the trappers always had a few tricks up their sleeves that they saved for fresh-faced, soon-to-be factors such as myself.

One time at my first posting, Ogoki Post, in 1979, an old trapper walked in eating little meaty spheres from a brown paper bag. He offered me one, which I accepted, as I wanted to blend in with the locals and be a bush guy. Just as I was about to pop the gooey morsel into my mouth, the manager, Kevin, slapped the cultural snack from my grasp, sending the meaty projectile across the office. "Don't eat that, you idiot!" he cried. "Don't you know what that is?"

"No, I don't," I said with surprise, as I was unaccustomed to having my meals slapped from my grasp.

"That is a beaver testicle! They are called castors or castoriums; we buy them by the pound wet or dry, just like we buy fur." The trapper, whose name was Archie, was now rolling on the floor laughing. He spoke only Ojibway but he understood perfectly what Kevin was saying by the look on my face.

Archie was the toughest man I ever met. He came to the post one time with his hand wrapped in a bloodied towel. He had sliced his palm open while skinning out a fox and had come in from his trapline for supplies and for medical attention. There was no medical attention available in Ogoki so he had come to the post. Unfortunately, the manager was elsewhere at the time. I cleaned the wound as best I could and then sewed up his hand with a needle and some fishing line. He did not even wince as I stitched him up. Now that is a tough guy, by any definition from the old neighbourhood in downtown Toronto.

When I was at Nakina Post in Ontario, the manager told me of the biggest fur scam of all time, even better than Archie's castorium joke. A new Hudson's Bay store had just been built there and the architect had the foresight to ventilate the fur room, which usually smelled like Canada Packers on Pork Day. His design called for a skylight to be installed on the ceiling of the room. A clever trapper, who had discovered the skylight worked in the same fashion as a cat flap in a door, formulated a cunning plan. Each evening, he would lower his five-year-old son through the skylight on a rope. The kid would then scoop up as many pelts as he could manage and then signal to be reeled in by his dad. The trapper would then sell the poached furs to the Bay the next day. After numerous nocturnal visits, the pair was caught, as the shipping inventory was discovered to be quite different from the purchasing ledger. Also, some of the furs started to become awfully familiar to the buyers.

In Portage La Loche, Saskatchewan, the trappers have been known to slip a skinned-out dog or two in with the coyotes in hopes that an inexperienced lad such as myself would be buying on that particular day. I was, they did, and six weeks later I received a nasty letter and debit note from Fur Central somewhere deep in the bowels of Hudson's Bay House. I shared my experience with the other clerks, or "trainees" as we were also known, in hopes that they would be spared the embarrassment I had experienced while on the fur learning curve.

When I finally found myself in Kugluktuk in the western Arctic, I thought I was at the pinnacle of my fur-trading career and wise to all the fur scams honed over the centuries. The Inuit would occasionally slip a huge Arctic hare pelt in with the foxes

Here I am using an axe to clear the ice from the surface of my ice fishing hole. Shortly after this picture was taken, the axe flew from my grip. It now rests on the bottom of Baker Lake. One must not underestimate how scarce axes are in arctic communities where there are no trees. (Baker Lake, NU, 1980)

and hope that I did not notice that the fur did not have a tail. I also kept a small black rug in my office over which I would shake each fox to ensure it had not been rolled in flour to enhance its whiteness.

That was how I met Samuel, a trader trying to sell me a fox that had been rolled in flour. He was an Inuit elder of poor dental health, but of great spirit. He came to visit me so frequently, I had to keep a supply of barge pilot biscuits and hot tea available at all times. I created a custom of serving tea and bickies to all of my trappers as they ritually stopped at the Bay, rather than at home, when returning from their traplines.

Sam would get his pension cheque near the end of each month and would invite himself for tea and bickies in my office while putting his "X" on the back of his cheque. The old man seemed to like my company; he began to bring his mail for me to read aloud to him. One day Sam asked me in broken English, "Can you show me how to make a John Henry?"

"What in the hell is a John Henry?"

Sam explained, "When I was a younger man, I used to bring all of my furs to the Bay. The manager back then said it was stupid for a grown man to write an "X" instead of being able to write his own John Henry. Nobody ever showed me how to make a John Henry. Will you teach me so I can write like the *kadloonok* do? If you do, I will bring you some *tuktoo* meat."

"What is a *tuktoo*?" I asked, thinking that there was no way there was a species of arctic creature about which I had not yet heard.

"Caribou meat," laughed Samuel.

"Okay, Sam, you have a deal!"

Sam spent many hours in my office over the following year, trying his hardest to write his name. We got to the point where he could duplicate his name if I wrote it down for him first, but he could not generate the signature on his own. I was feeling frustrated but did not reveal my frustration to Sam, as he was earnest, determined, and infinitely patient with this project. It seemed to be very important to him to be able to sign his name independently.

When it was time for me to leave Kugluktuk, Northwest Territories, for my next posting, my replacement removed the tea and bickies from my—his—office, as he felt it was inappropriate to be eating and drinking with our customers during business transactions. As it is with all snow gypsies, I was unable to say goodbye to everyone in the community. I was unable to bid farewell to Sam.

Most communities were used to the comings and goings of the Hudson's Bay personnel and learned to take them in stride. However, many elders had told me of the days when the

Hudson's Bay factor would settle in a community for an entire lifetime, marry a local girl, and raise a family. Letting go of my friends, the trappers, and leaving a community was always difficult for me. To this day, I remember all of the faces although the names escape me at times.

Many years later, while working on a project in Cambridge Bay, which is now known as Ikaluktutiak ("good fishing place"), I ran into one of Samuel's daughters. She told me that the old man had wept when he heard I had left. She also told me that soon after I left, he received his pension cheque in the mail, marched down to the Bay with it, and signed his name for the very first time, just like the white people do.

SPARK PLUGS

In the old days, when Hudson's Bay Company personnel signed on, they had multi-year contracts. If the factor in question were posted to the Arctic, he could count on not having any vacation time for several years. Originally a cost-saving measure, the policy also resulted in Company personnel learning the local dialect of the indigenous peoples. By the time I signed on with the company, it was the late 1970s, and the contracts were different. New factors challenged themselves to learn the local language for other reasons. I, however, really struggled with the languages I encountered.

In Kugluktuk, I was determined to try to learn at least basic Inuktitut so I would be able to converse with my customers and staff. I also wanted to know what the local folks were saying about their brand new baby-faced factor. After a few months, I thought I had a fairly good grasp of the elements of Inuktitut. I found that with just a few very basic words and phrases I was quite successful with communication, with my staff in particular. I was able to give simple instructions and carry out day-to-day commerce with the Inuit people.

As successful as I thought I was, there soon came a day when I was humbled. I thought that I knew the language well enough to know everything that was happening around me. I didn't. Once again I was reminded to watch quietly and learn. That is the way of the Inuit and the way they teach their children.

A wonderful young Inuit woman worked at the Bay in Kugluktuk. She was a good cashier and a very pleasant person. The only drawback was her annoying habit of frequently approaching me to ask if it was okay if she went home to change her spark plugs. It got to the point where I became quite cross with her and suggested she change her spark plugs on her own time. "We have work to do here!" Occasionally she would cry and say, "You're so mean. I liked our other manager better. Why did you have to come here?"

I would respond, "Well, I'm sorry, Shirley, that's the way things are. The old manager isn't here any longer. You're here with me, and if you want to keep your job, get back to work! Forget about changing your spark plugs!" I wondered why on earth somebody would ask to be excused from work to change his or her spark plugs.

After I had made short work of Shirley's bizarre request, I was surprised to hear from some of my other cashiers that they also wished to go home to change their spark plugs. I understood that the snowmobile had become just as important to the Inuit as their dog teams once were. And I also understood that it was very important to keep your snowmobile in good repair because, if you didn't, your life would be at risk out on the tundra. But *why* would somebody have to leave during the hours of work to change their spark plugs? I was sure there were able-bodied men folk back at home who could do the job. I decided that it was just a quirk that I would never understand. I decided to let the ridiculous issue rest. I had to focus on bigger things.

My area manager, who commuted two thousand kilometres from Edmonton every now and then, was coming for a visit and I wanted the store to look pretty spiffy as I was new to Kugluktuk and I had never met him. Also, I knew the area manager would want to spend a little time with each of the Inuit personnel. He would ask them how they were doing, but what he was really after was intelligence on what the manager was up to. It's difficult to supervise someone who is two thousand kilometres away.

Well, on this particular trip, the area manager must have heard from everybody in the store about how mean I was because I wouldn't let the women go home and change their spark plugs. My area manager took me to task on the issue as he lit up a cigarette while we sat in the coffee room.

He explained to me that he had been the area manager in this area for more than ten years and never had he had a manager upset everybody so soon after arriving and about something so trivial. "What is your problem, my friend?" he scolded. I responded that I didn't understand why they kept asking me if they could go home and change their spark plugs. The area manager didn't see why there was a problem; it wasn't a problem for any of the other managers. Everyone else seemed to be able to work around this; why should it be a problem for me? I sat quietly, thinking there had to be something here that wasn't right.

I asked my area manager, "Could you please explain this to me because I just don't get it." He asked if my parents had told me about the birds and the bees. "What have the birds and the bees to do with the Inuit changing their spark plugs?"

A look of realization came upon the area manager's face and he uttered a loud "*Ahhhhhhhh*," which was his particular "light bulb" noise. He explained that Inuktitut had a very basic vocabulary. It didn't have the words to identify the emerging technology and products that came with the white people now settling in the north. Many new items and ideas began to appear in the Inuit communities over a very short period of time. They moved from the Stone Age to the computer age in one generation. In an act of linguistic creativity, the Inuit decided to name the new objects flooding their communities according to the object's characteristics; they gave them the names of objects of similar characteristics that they already knew.

Tampons had recently been introduced to the selection of products available to the women of the community. To the Inuit, tampons looked very much like spark plugs, an item for which they did have a name. My staff had been asking me if they could please be excused from work so that they could go home and change their tampons, assuring me that they would be right back. I had missed the obvious, foolishly trusting in my newly acquired Inuktitut vocabulary and had offended my entire staff. I made my own "light bulb" noise, as it all suddenly became clear.

Fortunately, my Inuit employees were good-natured. They had a good laugh about it and then put all of the hard feelings away.

BLUEBERRY HILL

In the Arctic, the changing seasons alter the landscape completely. The snow gives way to a wonderful panorama of colourful mosses, lichens, and tiny, earth-hugging plants of every possible description. My favourite plant was what seems to be a little Q-Tip cotton ball sticking out of the earth; it appeared just about everywhere. The land was beautiful without snow, and I enjoyed going for long hikes across the bouncy tundra and watching the hic-hics, which are silly-looking ground squirrels. They are very much like gophers and can be seen bobbing their heads out of the earth here, there, and everywhere.

I was walking past the dump one day, crossing to an area behind Baker Lake called Blueberry Hill. Where I come from,

"Blueberry Hill" is a place where you make out in the back seat of your car. In Baker Lake, it is a hill on which blueberries grow. I thought I would see if the berries had ripened yet and had stuffed a plastic bag in my back pocket, thinking I would perhaps pick enough berries to make a pie. Suddenly, a group of Inuit teenagers came running toward me.

"Don't go over there!" they warned.

"*Akla*! *Akla*! There is a grizzly bear on Blueberry Hill!"

I corrected the young folks. "You mean a polar bear, don't you?"

"No, *nanook* lives to the north. There are no polar bears here! Run! Before *Akla* catches us all. They eat people!" I would later learn that there had been incidents resulting from lost grizzlies coming up the river and approaching the community.

I saw genuine fear in their eyes and thought it best to heed their advice. I joined the young lads who ran to the RCMP to report the bear. The constable grabbed a rifle from his lock-up and went over to the home of the Fish and Wildlife officer. The two men then summoned several of the local hunters and trappers in order to assemble a posse to hunt the bear. I decided to follow to see what was happening because I had never seen a grizzly bear, with the exception of the one in the Riverdale Zoo in Toronto. The urban grizzly had looked rather pitiful to me behind those bars. He was playing with a diaper and was down in his moat, running around in circles. I was excited about seeing one in the wild, seeing what its *grizzlyness* was all about.

We came to within a short distance of where the teenagers had seen the bear, then all lay down near the hilltop and slowly inched forward until we crested the hill. We looked down past a small valley to the area called Blueberry Hill. It was covered with blueberries. Sure enough, in the distance we could see a brown furry object bobbing up and down. We all crept closer, and I could see that the Inuit were getting very nervous. All of us civilians decided to hang back behind the two federal guys, who were being paid to face this kind of danger. Everybody crept forward in a small line until finally we were so close to the bear that I thought I could probably hit him with a rock.

Suddenly, the RCMP officer yelled, "Don't shoot! Don't shoot!"

Everybody relaxed his trigger finger, including me, and I didn't even have a gun. The bear stood up on his back legs, and I overheard a couple of the Inuit say, "That's not much of a bear, it looks pretty small."

The fearsome beast then raised its mighty head, and I noticed he was holding a bucket full of blueberries! The predator was now looking us right in the eye. It appeared to very closely resemble Martha, a plump village elder. She was wearing a fur coat from I don't know where. It looked as if it were made from beaver, which confused me as I had never seen a beaver in the Arctic. From what I understand of beavers, they need trees to survive.

The RCMP officer looked at the wildlife officer and both mopped the sweat off their faces. "We almost shot her," said the wildlife officer in a shaky voice.

Martha suddenly noticed all the eyes that had been watching her. Then she noticed the guns that were pointed in her direction. Putting two and two together, she came running across the field yelling something in Inuktitut that seemed to put the fear of God into everyone.

For some reason, everybody panicked and ran.

I couldn't understand why the men were so afraid of one little old lady. Just a minute ago, they were all prepared to sneak up on a huge grizzly bear and shoot it.

Martha quickly gave up the chase; her legs were short, and the men were running very fast. It turned out that the old lady, who was rumoured to be the daughter of a shaman, had threatened to put a curse on them for being foolish and pointing guns at her. I wandered down to the side of the hill to help her pick some berries so she could make blueberry bannock for her family.

GRANDPA'S
WOODPILE

The average Hudson's Bay Company trainee could count on being transferred several times before becoming a manager. Then, as a manager, one would most certainly be transferred many more times during the course of a career with the Honourable Company. All that moving around was difficult at times, but it allowed for my personal exploration of northern Canadian geography and aboriginal cultures. It also allowed me to discover one constant in the communities I encountered during my travels. The HBC was widely known as "The Horny Boys Club."

Let's think about this for a minute: young men, away from

home or country for the first time. Then, consider the setting: tiny, remote villages, populated by young women from the first generation of their community to discover television and the outside world it portrayed. It was the typical small-town scenario. "The grass is always greener, anywhere else but here."

In the 1970s and 1980s, the Bay recruited its employees from areas of Canada with high rates of unemployment. The Company also continued to recruit Scotsmen from the Orkneys as they were hearty, intelligent, and ambitious souls, despite their short arms and deep pockets. There did not seem to be too much difficulty in recruiting Canadian lads, and yet it seemed the company was unable to keep the recruits for any length of time.

During my years with the Bay, I believe I set some sort of company record for quitting and then being rehired, certainly more times than anyone else in the company's three-hundred-year history. During this time, I had the opportunity to observe many of my fellow factors have relationships with Native women from the communities. The company had always looked the other way when its factors took "bush wives" or "country wives" as they were once known. Even in present times, many such relationships were of convenience and not formed out of love or goodwill. Most of these relationships were hard on the Native women as their factor husbands often used them as slaves and bedwarmers. In many cases, even this situation was much more comfortable for the women than a life in the bush. However, Native women are committed to their extended families. Bay men were frequently transferred. The breaking up of the extended family was difficult for these women to bear. Also, their children were often sent out of the communities to southern schools.

This is not to say that many of the relationships between Bay men and Native women were not tender and earnest in the beginning. Many of the recruits from the Maritimes married Inuit women, then quit the company and moved home, bringing their wives with them. Most of those relationships did not seem to survive as the young men did not take into account the strong cultural and family ties many Inuit women have to their home communities. Isolated culturally and linguistically, many Inuit women wilted, longing for their homeland. The foods they were accustomed to were not available, and southern Canadian culture was guided by completely different standards for both child rearing and work ethic. I'm sure some of these Company– community unions have survived; I'm just not aware of any.

However, the relationships forged between Inuit women and young men who decided to stay in the northern community fared much better. There were, of course, many struggles to overcome in that scenario as well. Whether or not the relationships managed to work themselves out, in my view it was the children of such unions who faced the biggest challenges. They were considered neither Native nor white. They hadn't any of the benefits of the Native culture and felt the scorn and racism of white people.

Kevin was a jovial east coast Canadian who became a factor and let it go to his head. He became bossy, demanding, and very set in his ways. He had only been with the company one year longer than I. Kevin married a Cree woman in northern Ontario and chose to remain in her home community. He had a wonderful relationship with his spouse; they had two children. Kevin embraced the Cree people and learned much from them. It made him a better man and a better Bay manager. In time, Kevin was offered a promotion to a larger post in a nearby Cree community.

He realized that if he rejected a transfer his progress within the company would most likely be halted forever. After consultation with his wife and her family, it was decided that they should move to ensure a comfortable future for themselves. The small family did very well over the next two years; Kevin's sons were then three and four years of age. They had been raised as non-Native children despite having had some exposure to their mother's language and culture.

The young boys missed many sensible lessons that they would have learned had they been with their mother's extended family, basic lessons that non-Native parents would not consider teaching, such as staying away from chained dogs and not handling firearms or ever pointing a gun at another person. For safety, aboriginal children learn to respect fire, the weather, and the danger of being out on the water or ice.

After two years in the new post, Kevin and his family took a three-week vacation to visit the boys' grandparents, who had not seen them since they had moved. The reunion was joyous, and the children basked in the attention of their aunts, uncles, cousins, and grandparents. Silas, the younger of the two boys, asked many questions and was fascinated with all the new things that surrounded him. He helped his grandpa pull in the fishnets and cut wood, and he laughed when he almost fell through the hole when using an outhouse for the first time. It was a special time for all of them, and Kevin, seeing the joy in his wife's and children's faces, began to feel regret for putting his aspirations with the company ahead of his family's needs.

On the second week of the visit, Silas went missing. The entire community rallied to search for the missing boy. The search continued until darkness set in. It was then that Silas's grandfather, while preparing the evening fire to warm the house, discovered the tiny boy's body buried beneath the woodpile, which had collapsed on him when he had tried to climb it.

The entire community mourned for Silas and his distraught parents. He was buried amongst his ancestors, beneath a birch tree by the river. Grandpa had few words at the burial and fewer still for his young daughter, of whom he was so proud for marrying a Hudson's Bay man. He would miss the young boy for the rest of his days. Grandpa did not see his grandson as Cree or white, he saw him as a grandson. He chose to remain silent because he knew that a Cree child would have known better than to go climbing on the woodpile, to show off to his grandpa.

The lesson is the same now as it was in the 1700s. The progeny of Bay men and Native women struggle for identity. They are part of each culture, but somehow end up as neither. They have problems being accepted by both cultures and often pay dearly for not being entirely a part of one culture or the other.

THE GREAT NECESSITY

In 1980, I received very sound advice from an unlikely source. I had just bought a camera with my first paycheque from the Hudson's Bay Company and had been making a nuisance of myself around the community of Baker Lake. I believed I was living through the end of an era and felt I had a duty to record it.

Joe was one of the first Inuit elders I met in the north who spoke English just as well as I did. He took me aside one day as I was preparing to price and restock some eggs that had been stored at room temperature and were ready to hatch at any moment. He told me that the people in the community were getting annoyed with me for constantly sticking a camera in their faces, even when they were shopping at the Bay. He pointed out

155

that if I really wanted to get to know the people I should lose the camera and get myself a snowmobile. Coincidentally, Joe just happened to have an old snowmobile for sale.

Three weeks and four hundred bucks later, I finally got my "new" snowmobile running. I asked Joe if I could go on a hunting trip with him in order to try out my new ride. Ever the wise elder, Joe advised me that it would be foolhardy to attempt to take my hunk-of-junk sled across the tundra. Besides, he would be busy photographing his nephew's wedding that weekend with his new camera. However, Joe did feel he should be the one to take me on my first hunting trip and that he should start by offering me some advice about hunting on the land. He agreed to meet me at the staff house later that day.

When I arrived home from work, I found Joe waiting for me, sipping on his sugary tea and dipping his barge pilot biscuit. He decided to share with me some grandfatherly advice with regard to being a white guy exploring the Arctic tundra.

Don't.

"Have you ever ridden on a snowmobile before?" he asked.

"No."

"Have you ever killed anything before?"

"That depends what you mean by *kill*, Joe," I responded.

Somewhat amused, but also annoyed, Joe made a number of suggestions designed to prepare me to accompany him out on the land, on a yet-to-be-determined date. The old man observed that killing was wrong, but it was part of "the Great Necessity." The Inuit have survived on the barren land for unknown millennia. Hunters have to kill to feed their families. "Our people kill only what we need to survive; killing for any other reason is wrong. Not only is senseless killing wrong, it throws the land and all that live on it out of balance. You must respect the land, the animals, and the people who live here," Joe said. Then he asked an important question. "Do you really need to hunt?"

"I want to understand your people, Joe, and I want to understand life and death. I want your people to understand me."

"You sound like one of those white people who stays here for a week and then goes home and writes a book," Joe chastised me. "No, Joe, I'm different, really," I whined.

Finishing his tea and scooping the sugary sludge from the bottom of his cup, Joe put his mug into the sink and ran some water into it. He then suggested I take a couple of weeks to test drive my snowmobile, get some experience on the land, and find out how reliable it was going to be. He also suggested I take my .22 magnum rifle and practise so I would be able to pull my weight on a hunting trip. Fair enough, I thought. I agreed it would be better if no one else was around while I honed my arctic hunting skills. I knew Joe liked to tease me and to play little jokes on me, but I sensed he was being honest, if not fatherly, as he instructed me in the philosophy of "the Great Necessity."

Saturday morning I awakened early, gassed my machine, and set out for the cluster of hills just west of the community. I left my homemade komatik (of Irish design) behind as it had fallen apart on its maiden trip the previous evening. My objective was to go rabbit hunting in order to prove to Joe that city boys, specifically white Irish guys, make great hunters.

I shared the Hudson's Bay Company staff house with two Newfoundlanders who seemed to be more interested in tracking the indigenous females than hunting. They both agreed, however, that it would be nice to have "a right good feed of rabbit stew" and wished me luck.

I rode my trusty machine over those hills and started to get a feel for how it handled. It was a glorious and sunny spring day, not very cold, and I congratulated myself on being such an avid explorer and adventurer on this Arctic frontier. I stopped when I thought I had discovered a valley where no white man had ever trod. Digging into my pack, I removed three plastic snowmobile oil containers that I had brought along for target practice. I counted off fifty paces and proceeded to snipe at the helpless vessels. Two hundred rounds later, I felt I had the hang of this hunting/shooting gig. Just as I was walking over to pick up my now decimated plastic targets, a rabbit, or more correctly, an Arctic hare, shot by me, moving faster than any living thing I had ever seen. What a cheeky little critter, I thought. I did not even have time to raise my rifle.

The hunt was on.

I followed the mobile meal for over an hour. I was on foot and tired quickly as the hare dragged me up and down hill after hill. I followed his tracks in the snow and noticed that he was far enough ahead of me to periodically stop and make little rabbit jelly beans. I soon began to feel that the piles of poop my prey was scattering were meant to mock me. I continued.

Stopping to catch my breath, I spotted my nemesis casually sunning himself by an outcropping of jagged rock, no doubt planning his next move. I fired twice and heard the bullets ricochet off the rock face. The hare disappeared. But I was determined to catch him. I found myself wandering those hills all afternoon; I would track down that robust, rascally rabbit.

It was getting late, and I was beginning to consider finding my way back to the snow machine to head home. Looking around to get my bearings, I spotted the hare feeding on some sort of sage grass that was protruding from beneath the snow, right next to my snowmobile.

I raised my rifle and fired.

I heard a slapping sound as the bullet struck the rabbit, sending him tumbling down the side of the hill. When I caught up to him, he was still alive and bleeding from a wound in his chest. His back legs were making a rapid running motion as he struggled to draw a breath. I looked into his eyes and saw the brightness and sharp hue of his orbs fade to gray as the life left his body.

Suddenly the rabbit became still. All became quiet. The only sounds I could hear were that of my own heartbeat and of the wind coming in from the lake and finding a route through the rocky hills.

I had not expected to have to watch as the creature I had chased all day took his last breath. And I had certainly not expected to feel the way I did about taking the life of another creature. I should have been elated; I had won, after all. That is what I had learned on the streets of Toronto: Go for it! Be a winner. But I found no joy in killing the rabbit, and I did not

We did not do much rabbit hunting where I grew up in downtown Toronto. However, I received instruction from the Inuit elders in the community and quickly became a crack shot and all round good hunter. I chased this rabbit for an entire day and finally bagged him when he stopped to poop and I bushwhacked him from upwind. (Baker Lake, NU, 1980)

understand what was going on inside of me. I brought the meat back for my roommates so that they could make stew. Those two knuckleheads would have been just as pleased if I had brought home a box of Kraft Dinner.

In time, I realized that on that beautiful and sunny day, I had taken the first step toward understanding the Inuit people and "the Great Necessity," which was part of their lives, and of mine. Joe, in his own Inuit way, had let me discover "the Great Necessity" for myself. With few words, he had taught me a life lesson that his people had known for millennia.

CONFESSING TO FATHER CAT

When the Hudson's Bay Company first came to the Arctic, it was accompanied by the RCMP and Catholic and/or Anglican missions, and later, a nursing station. The first buildings to appear in most communities were erected to house the immigrants from the south and warehouse their needs. They also all required a place to conduct their business: that of God, that of the Crown, and the somewhat loftier business of The Gentlemen and Adventurers of England Trading into Hudson Bay.

In short order, the Inuit moved in closer to see what the strange folks were up to and to determine where all the right-angled igloos had come from. Later, after everyone knew who was boss, a school or two popped up in order to help the aboriginals figure out the only thing on their land that made no sense to them.

The Catholic Church, being one of the first arrivals in the Arctic communities, sent an assortment of priests from many different European locations. The most numerous fathers found in the north were the Oblate missionaries who had come from France.

The first parishes built in the Arctic communities during the early days of the 1930s, '40s, and '50s were hand-built by the hearty immigrant missionaries. One of the priests with whom I became well acquainted in Hall Beach was an Oblate missionary, Father Lechat, known to the local people as Father Cat. The name was much easier to pronounce for the Inuit and well described the rotund, gentle, and loving man of God. Father was loved and respected by everyone in the community. He had taken the time to learn the language of the people and had always respected their ways.

Father Lechat was a great storyteller in any language. On the many occasions I found myself sharing a meal with him, storytelling would ensue. Father's tales became more and more outrageous as he went along. Fortunately for him, not many people were around at the time, thus creating a lack of reliable witnesses to confirm or deny his claims. It was from Father Lechat that I gained my perspective in storytelling. He had told me many stories, each beginning with, "I don't know if this story is the truth, but this is how I remember it."

When Father Cat first arrived in Hall Beach on the Fox Basin from France, he set about learning English and the local dialect of Inuktitut, which was quite different from the Inuktitut spoken in the central Arctic, Keewatin, or western Arctic. The local people there speak a dialect that is a synthesis of all the dialects spoken on Baffin Island. He also sought to make his church accessible to his congregation and their way of life, as was obvious in the manner in which he approached the subject of confession during *egonuk* season in Hall Beach.

Hall Beach is on the mainland, one hundred and thirty kilometres south of Igloolik, hugging the shoreline. The beaches that border both communities are large expanses of gravel and are quite soft and easy to excavate. The Inuit would dig huge pits in the beaches in order to cache meat. The process of hunting and caching meat has been going on for many years and is still happening today.

The people living at Hall Beach hunt walrus because there is a massive polynia (an area of Arctic Ocean that never freezes over) just a mile or so off the coast. The hunters bring the stinky walrus to the beach after shooting or harpooning them. The unfortunate marine mammal is then gutted, butchered, and stuffed back into its own skin. The finished product resembles a giant, three-hundred-kilogram sausage when tied off at both ends. The mega-sausage is then placed in a deeply dug pit in the gravel; the gravel is filled in and a stick with a flag on it stuck in the beach. The meat lies beneath the gravel to decay and ferment for one entire year, at which point a hungry posse with the constitution of billy goats digs it up and deposits a new Inuit *kielbasa* beneath the surface. The local folks called the rotten walrus *egonuk*.

One day in 1992, I foolishly volunteered to take a boat trip with a family, as they needed some sturdy lads with big arms to help lift their enormous takeout order of sausage. The best part was taking the odiferous behemoth back to the community, standing downwind all the way whilst retching over the gunnels of the boat. We just picked up one sausage that day, and it took us half the day to drag the thing across the beach and get it up to the boat, by rolling it up a ramp. The rotting meat smelled like Limburger cheese on steroids.

One of the Inuit elders aboard showed me that it helped to break the filters off a couple of cigarettes and stuff them up your nose to reduce the stench. I followed suit; unfortunately, I couldn't seem to get a tight seal around the filters. Cursing the Roman invaders of my parents' Irish homeland for their contribution of large nose genes to the gene pool, I remained overwhelmed by the stench of rotting meat.

We succeeded in placing the delicacy across the bow to keep the front of our craft down and balance the boat. All the Native passengers sat in the back of the boat, backs to the fouled Arctic wind, feasting on the bloody entrails of the new walrus, which now occupied his own skin as a sausage casing. When we got back to Sanarijak (as the Inuit called their community), we rolled the giant sausage onto the town beach to the cheers of the local folks, who had come down to see the arrival of the first quantity of ripe *egonuk* of the season. The people of the community shared everything.

Several elders came forward to ritually carve up the feast with a snow-knife that was also known as a *punaat*, or igloo-building knife. I thought the stench had been bad when the thing was an intact sausage. That odour had only been a preview and held nothing in comparison to the stench that filled the air when the sausage casing was punctured with the snow-knife. People started taking huge unwieldy chunks, larger than their children. Garbage bags were the new Tupperware, as all were dashing home with their share of the wondrous delicacy to share with their families. *Egonuk* was a seasonal treat and was rare once the orgy was over. The Inuit would find themselves longing for a taste of the rapturous rot, as an entire year would have to pass before it was available again.

After my trip to dig up the walrus sausage, and after watching the *egonuk* frenzy that ensued, I spoke with Father Lechat, who told me his own story about the delicacy. It seemed that when the mission was new, it had included a standard confessional. This changed when Father found that the air in the confessional became polluted during *egonuk* season. If someone who had eaten *egonuk* came to the confessional, he or she would spew *egonuk* breath. Father would begin dry heaving between sins, and, on several occasions, he had to excuse himself in the middle of the confession and dash to the rectory to make his contribution to the porcelain. Father contacted another priest at the parish in

Igloolik, which was just up the coast, for assistance.

The priest at Igloolik agreed that Catholic faithful fouling the confessional with toxic *egonuk* breath simply would not do. The priest from Igloolik asked Father Cat about whether he had made any progress in persuading the Inuit, who ate only meat, to give up the eating of meat on Fridays. No. In their brainstorming session both men of the cloth also determined that the use of incense during mass failed to cover up the breath of the worshipping multitudes. They also discussed holding mass outdoors during *egonuk* season, à la St. Francis of Assisi. It was argued that St. Francis would have most likely objected to one of God's wondrous creatures, the walrus, being humiliated and made into a lowly sausage.

In the end, having reached no solution, Father Lechat joined forces with the other priest and talked to the Bishop of the Arctic diocese. A special dispensation from the Holy See must have been granted; the confessional came down, giving way to group absolution during mass. The idea also seemed to please the Inuit. I do not know what happened with the issue of eating meat on Fridays. I know that although the Inuit loved their caribou and walrus meat, the next favourite thing was raw, frozen fish. I don't think God would have minded that. His own Son, after all, had spent his life as a Fisher of Men.

STOVEPIPES, WIRE BRUSHES, AND OTHER WAYS TO FEED YOUR FAMILY

One of the most remarkable things I discovered on my many journeys in the Arctic was the ingenuity and will to survive of the Native people. I was always delighted when the people of any community would accept me and take me out on the land where they could show me what was unfolding out there. The Native people were proud of their knowledge and willing to share it. They were the "managers in charge," once we were outside the front doors of the local Hudson's Bay store. I enjoyed learning some pretty crafty survival techniques from the community elders and wondered how the people had come up with such ideas.

An old man named Drummer dropped by the staff house in Sandy Lake, Ontario, early on a Sunday morning. He wanted to go chicken hunting. (To me, chicken was something ordered by the bucket. I was to discover that when the Cree said "chicken," what they meant was grouse.) I was puzzled as the gentlemen who were going out with Drummer had arrived with two pairs of snowshoes and no rifle.

"How are we going to get chickens without a rifle?" I asked.

"You'll see," they said.

Drummer only shook his head.

Off we went.

I put a couple of chocolate bars and a can of sardines into my pocket, just in case. I had learned to take that little precaution from the people long ago. I always carried extra food with me in a cold environment. One could always build a fire in the area where I was posted at the time, with all of the trees around, but one cannot last very long without food.

I pulled up on the rusted-out old Company snow machine behind Drummer as we approached an area on the backside of a hill, which was on the west side of the lake. The elder gentlemen told me that this area had been part of Drummer's family trapline when he was a little boy.

We planned to walk the length of the unused trapline so that they could show me the various places where Drummer had hung out when they were growing up in the bush with their families. I was happy to hear the stories, which all the men seemed to be starving to tell. Since television had been introduced into the communities, the young men were more concerned with the women they had seen on TV and with keeping up with the styles and images the new media dictated to them. There was no longer much interest in learning from the elders of the community.

The skills that had accumulated, and that were to be shared, were honed over many generations. Yet in a single generation they could be lost. I had had my fill of TV as a child and was keen to be taken under the collective wings of these old guys. The elders, in turn, were thankful for an audience. Even though I was a white man, I was willing to learn. It was hurtful to the older folks that many of their own people were not interested in continuing the traditional knowledge of the people.

As we walked on the trapline, I suddenly noticed that every half-kilometre or so there seemed to be a shiny piece of stovepipe shoved down into the snow.

"What's with the pipe?" I asked Drummer.

The old man had trouble understanding me, as he spoke mostly Cree, and I spoke only English. I pantomimed my interest in the pipes and Drummer took the time to show me what he was doing with them.

The Cree people learned to use everything they found in their environment. That includes junk brought onto their land by white people arriving with "progress." Retrieving useful materials from the HBC, RCMP, and nursing station dumps for generations had made the Cree people the earliest recyclers on the continent.

Drummer produced a slick, half-metre length of stovepipe from his pack. It was black in colour, and he easily assembled it, then shoved it down into the snow. He then reached into his pocket, where he had a box of raisins, and dropped a handful of raisins into the bottom of the pipe.

"For the chickens," someone said.

"For the chickens? What does that mean?" I asked.

We walked quietly as we proceeded farther up the trapline. Drummer stopped occasionally in order to set up more of his raisin-powered stovepipes. After walking about five kilometres through the snow without snowshoes, I was ready to begin complaining about being wet. Drummer suddenly reversed our course. Following our own tracks, with me in the lead, the old man veered away and signalled that he would meet me at the camp, where he and his geriatric entourage would have a fire. Pleased that Drummer trusted me to be alone in the bush, I stayed on our trail, checking the stovepipes on my return trip.

Without exception, every stovepipe contained a fat little chicken! The greedy little guys had gone for the raisins, reached too far into the pipe, and slid to the bottom headfirst. They were trapped, unable to turn around or back out because of their over-sized back ends. Lunch! I concluded that the Cree were masters of bird psychology and all that involved raisins. I arrived at camp with a full game bag to be greeted by a smiling old man who had taught me a lesson without having said a single word.

The master bushman then showed me how to stand on the chicken's wings, grab their legs, and pull, pluck, and skin the little guys in one stroke. Presto! Sitting in the palm of my hand was a perfectly dressed little piece of poultry to roast on the fire. We ate three chickens each, which was just enough. Then I had a hot cup of soup while Drummer and his buddies had their tea and biscuits. I had developed the habit of carrying packets of soup from my days amongst the ritual tea-drinking Inuit.

We watched the sun set and walked back to the community in the darkness. I had a lot of thinking to do, so it was good that none of my companions had anything else to say that day. They were all busy chewing snuff and spitting tobacco juice onto their own boots. Reflecting on Drummer's genius, I was ashamed that I had misread the people who were hosting me on their land.

No one in the community seemed to know who had thought up or learned their remarkable survival skills and adaptability. Things had just always been the way they were, and the people had always been here. No one questioned it or saw any reason to.

Later, I was to observe a host of other survival tricks from the Cree. In time, I learned to set snares for rabbits. The people laughed as I struggled to catch a rabbit but ended up trapping every imaginable critter in the woods, other than the rabbit.

One clever old man used to take a wire brush and pluck some of the wires. The needle-like bristle would then be passed through a raisin. After making a handful of the little raisin booby traps, he would scatter them in the bush. Returning several hours later, he would find small piles of chickens lying everywhere, having gagged on the wire while trying to scarf down the raisins. Lunch would be lying there, just waiting to be picked up and cooked. The meat was kept fresh by the coldness of the snow, ready for the campfire. That is, if the foxes or ravens didn't get there first. Ingenious.

In the Native communities, no one need ever be hungry, cold, or unwanted. The people adapted to the changes that were forced on them. Sadness and loss overcomes me when I think of how much like us aboriginal Canadians have become and how few of their ways have found a place in our lives.

FOR THE LOVE
OF BOBBY

Once I had been in Kugluktuk for a few months, the Inuit employees at the Bay forgot the fact that I was not one of their people, well, most of the time. They would let their hair down and literally "chew the fat" with me. Whenever *muktuk,* or whale flesh, was available in the community, my staff would bring it to share as a snack at coffee time. They enjoyed watching me grimace as I chewed the fat with them, trying to show them that I was hip with all things Inuit. I hoped my efforts to be culturally sensitive would pay off, as whale blubber did not agree with my Irish entrails.

Over several years with the company, I had thrown out most of what I had known of personnel management. I replaced the inapplicable knowledge with a philosophy of learning to get the job done with what and whom I had to work with. If a manager tried to force his will on a community or on the people therein, he would quickly find himself looking for a new vocation. The Inuit did not use watches or calendars. They had blended with the seasons instead of fighting the elements and had survived where others would never have had a chance. Once I learned to flow with a community and operate a business within the rhythms of the local culture, I discovered success. The difficult part was meeting the demands, protocols, and expectations of the company and work within the Inuit philosophy.

When the weather was good and the ducks and geese were on the move, the staff would not show up for work. When the seals appeared on the sea ice in spring, the entire community would disappear for the seal hunt. At breakup time, everyone would be putting his boat into the water and would not have time to tend to his job. If a hunter were overdue and lost on the land or sea, every able-bodied person would be out searching or sitting by the radio waiting for news of the missing party. As a business operator, I had to learn to work around such events; the company was my priority, their lives and families were the Inuit people's first priority. I did not realize at first that I was learning from these people, that I, too, would rediscover my priorities and find a more fulfilling life.

The Inuit live closer to death than I ever had. Growing up in downtown Toronto, there was always someone dying somewhere, but I wasn't that close to it. People jumping onto the subway tracks were mere headlines. Traffic fatalities were so common that no one paid much attention to them. Deaths from crime were frequent but only allotted a few minutes on the evening news. A death in a tiny, remote community such as Kugluktuk touched everyone. The Inuit mourn as they live, with all of their beings. I, too, was touched when we lost an elder or community member or, worse yet, a child. In time, I learned how the Inuit dealt with death and found my way to an understanding of it, with their kindness and guidance. The community would almost shut down during a time of bereavement. After the burial, the entire community would rebound quickly and get on with life. To the Inuit, life and death were two sides of the same coin; one could not exist without the other.

On most mornings in Kugluktuk, I would unlock the store but leave the lights off so that my staff could get into the building. One morning, I lost track of time and noticed that it was a full half-hour after our usual opening time and no staff had yet arrived. I turned on the lights and probed the sales floor. No one. I looked outside and there wasn't a single person in sight. The weather wasn't very good, so I knew that it wasn't a "community hunting holiday." Concerned, I locked up the store and went to the RCMP detachment to find out what was happening. Either someone was lost on the land or there had been a death in the community.

The RCMP corporal was as confused as I. He would be the first person contacted if a search and rescue needed to be coordinated. We phoned the nursing station, where the nurse in charge was puzzling over where all her staff were. No one had died or surely the nursing station would know about it. I offered to knock on a few doors in order to ascertain what was going on.

My office assistant lived near the RCMP post, so I stopped there first. I knocked. No answer. I walked up the hill to my grocery clerk's house, where after my vigorous knocking, a teary-eyed woman answered the door.

"What's going on?" I asked.

The young woman burst into heartbreaking sobs and ran from the door back into the house. Someone has died, I thought. My grocery clerk then came to the still open door, tucking his T-shirt into a ridiculous pair of Superman boxers.

"Hi," he said with his eyes downcast. "I guess you've heard the bad news."

"What *bad news*?" I asked with a raised voice.

"Bobby died last night," he whispered.

"Bobby? Bobby who?" I asked in frustration.

"Bobby Ewing! I won't be into work today." Then he closed the door in my face.

Bobby Ewing?

It seems that the Inuit were so immersed in the evening soap opera *Dallas* that they had failed to realize that the characters on their television screens were fictional. Bobby Ewing had died the previous evening, and the local folks had accorded him the same respect and response that any other member of the community would have received on their demise.

I reported back to the RCMP detachment, where the nurse was now enjoying a coffee with the corporal. I filled them in and we were all too stunned to laugh. We all realized that we had not done the Inuit any favours by introducing them to television.

TOBACCO MAN

It was wise of the Hudson's Bay Company to choose one staff house design and build a lot of them. The most common staff house design was called a 12-DB. No one ever explained to me what "12-DB" meant. It was difficult transferring from one end of the country to the other; someone was always saying goodbye and few friendships had much chance of flourishing. That's where the houses served me well. Wherever I was posted, I found myself at home; I was in the same house. I recall times when I would wake up, know that I was at home in my little house, but not remember what community I was in. To this day I can spot a Hudson's Bay Company building from a plane at three thousand metres.

The first couple of days after arriving at a new posting, I always spent a few hours setting the staff house up to be as close as possible, on the interior, as the one I had just left. Keep in mind that the dwellings were "turnkey." The sheets were on the beds, fully furnished, curtains, you name it; it was already waiting there for us. The post manager always shopped at the Bay (of course), so most of the furnishings, appliances, and other comforts were also identical from community to community. I should not neglect to mention that there was always an abundance of traditional HBC point blankets in every home; we were never cold.

One morning at the Sandy Lake, Ontario, post, I dragged myself out of bed to tidy the house in anticipation of a visit by my area manager. The sun had not yet risen, and I thought I would take the opportunity to watch it rise over the treetops. Between me and the sunrise lay a rustic old cabin, whose lone occupant was standing on his porch waiting for the same sun as I was. I found myself watching the elder man rather than the sun as he seemed to be talking to someone who was not there. He took some tobacco from a pouch, and at first I thought he was going to roll himself a smoke before he went to split some firewood. He proceeded to rub the tobacco leaves between his fingers and then drop it on the ground. "Great," I thought. "I'm living next to a nut."

As the months spun by, I enjoyed many fishing and hunting trips with the Cree people. They didn't seem to mind that I was not one of their own, and they taught me much about the lake, the land, and the local creatures. Whenever I found occasion to rise early, regardless of the weather or season, my old neighbour was out there, talking to no one and wasting his smokes. By that time, I knew the elder as the fellow who had fishing nets under the lake ice just a kilometre from the river. But I wanted to know more about him and my curiosity got the better of me.

One spring morning, I walked over to get an unobstructed view of the sunrise and to introduce myself to my eccentric neighbour. I had learned a little Cree from my co-workers and hunting companions and thought that I might have a good chance of communicating with the old man. He nodded to acknowledge my presence and then proceeded to chant as he wasted more tobacco and offered me a pinch. I declined as I did not chew or smoke. But I wanted to know him better so after a quick game of charades, I was on the back of the old guy's toboggan, headed for the middle of the lake to help him pull in his nets.

For quite a few weeks, it became routine for me to get up early on Sundays to help Percy pull in the nets, harvest and sort his catch, and then reset the nets. I learned much from the old man. He seemed eager to share his skills but had no one to share them with. It worked for me.

Percy died the following spring. I heard about his death from the new manager of Sandy Lake. I was working at a nearby post and had frequently asked after him. Percy's son, Raymond, lived in the community where I was then buying fur, and I thought it right that I seek him out and share his grief as a friend of his father's. Raymond had not yet heard the news and struggled to compose himself in front of his family. I was invited to visit with Raymond's family before they departed for Sandy Lake by boat to attend the old man's funeral.

I gave Raymond a pouch of tobacco to leave with his dad as he was buried. Native people frequently send off their loved ones with some of their belongings. Many aboriginal people believe that life continues elsewhere and that, in starting a new life, the dead will require their most valued possessions. We exchanged stories of the old man. Raymond was amused by the fact that his father had enjoyed a friendship with a Hudson's Bay man, despite the fact that we did not share a common language. It hadn't occurred to me that Percy and I had never exchanged a word during our friendship. He was a silent man and there was no need. Despite our silence, I had learned much from the patient and generous man.

Raymond's family all laughed when I told them that I once fell into the fishing hole while helping Percy. They laughed about the pike that bit on my finger until Percy pried it off with his chainsaw file. Raymond's wife said she was glad that the old man had found a friend, as she had always worried about him being lonely.

I arose to leave as the family had to set out on their trip to Sandy Lake. But there was still one thing I did not understand about Percy and felt I had to ask. "Percy used to stand outside his cabin and talk to himself every morning. He also used to waste his tobacco all over the place, on the ground, into the lake; I even saw him throw a handful into our campfire once."

Raymond put his hand on my shoulder as we walked to the dock.

"My dad greeted the sun every morning, thanking it for rising and warming the land, bringing life. He wasn't talking to himself; he was singing a traditional song of thanks. Tobacco is sacred to the Cree; he was not wasting it. He thanked the lake for providing him with fish by sharing his tobacco. He thanked the earth for bringing him caribou, and he fed the fire tobacco to give thanks for the provision of food for himself and for you. He learned that from his grandfather; that has been the way of things since the beginning."

Percy was teaching me of things that I did not yet have the eyes to understand.

When the sun rose the following morning, I was there on the beach to watch it. In silent prayer I thanked the sun for coming back to us, for bringing us another day. I sprinkled some tobacco into the gentle waves that were lapping at the shore, making my peace with Percy's journey. I thanked the land and my God for every moment I had been given with that beautiful and silent old man of few but many words.

ALICE'S
HINDQUARTERS

Having grown up in downtown Toronto, I arrived in the north with my own complete set of gender biases. Most of what I knew, or thought I knew, got tossed rather quickly after my arrival in the northern aboriginal communities of Canada. At resupply time in the Arctic, for example, it was next to impossible to hire strong young men to help unload the barge, so we would hire women. The men had tasted high wages on the oil rigs and now would not work for less. This created manpower shortages everywhere.

In the old days, the entire community would turn out to

greet the barge; resupply time was a most festive occasion that marked the new year on the Arctic coast. Women, children, elders, everyone in the community lined up in chain gangs to pass the supplies from the barge up the beach to the Hudson's Bay Company warehouses. The Inuit were not paid for their labours; the supplies were for them.

These days, the company pays the local folks to move the freight to the warehouses. When I arrived on the scene in the 1980s, the barges were carrying their own forklifts and cargo containers. The containers were dropped in front of the appropriate warehouse, and a much smaller crew was required to move the goods indoors and stack them into tiers. The young guys were not interested in the work; they felt that menial labour and low pay were beneath them. So we hired women, young and old; they were strong, reliable, and not afraid of getting their hands dirty. I have witnessed elderly Inuit women, barely five feet in height, hoist huge bales of canvas or duffel that I could hardly lift myself.

The Cree women of northern Saskatchewan also filled all the positions at many posts. There was no such thing as a stockboy or any other designation of male gender-specific workers. The women did anything—mental or physical—that they put their minds to, including some pretty cunning work.

In Portage La Loche, Saskatchewan, the Hudson's Bay Company post was huge and even had its own butcher shop. I found it unusual that we sold enough meat to warrant having a butcher on staff. In most Native communities I lived in, the hunters took what they needed from the land as moose, caribou, and fish were plentiful.

Gordie, the butcher, was a diminutive Newfoundlander of great intensity. He was a perfectionist and wielded his many blades with the finesse of a samurai warrior. Gordie had one problem, though. Try as he may, he seemed to be unable to get the butcher shop to turn a profit. In fact, his sales results were so dismal, he was ordered to do weekly inventories of his meat locker in order to diagnose the problem.

It was at one such inventory that I met Alice. I had seen Alice around, but since I was working on the dry goods side of the massive store, I had little to do with her. She was one of the quiet ones. The store in Portage La Loche had more employees than any other post where I have ever worked. Alice spent most of her time helping out in the butcher shop, which seemed to have been glued onto the back of the store as an afterthought.

I had offered to assist Gordie with his meat inventory so he could finish quickly and attend the hockey game with me. Alice was the post janitor. She was a quiet little woman who was as wide as she was tall. She was a hard worker who raised and supported her many children on her own, and I instantly respected her.

Alice made some extra cash working as the store janitor on weekends. She was the only person in her extended family with a job. She carried a lot of weight on her shoulders. None of us had the courage to attempt to clean the butcher shop. She attacked the task with gusto.

Alice cleaned other areas of the post while we worked. When we finished the inventory, it was Alice's cue to descend on the butcher shop and clean every square inch. We headed out to watch the game.

At the hockey game that night, we met a group of brothers from the Catholic mission located across from the store. I greeted the brothers politely and received a snub for my trouble. I wondered what was going on as I had not even been introduced to these bush monks.

"You young men are very lazy," one of the brothers sniffed.

"I'm willing to wager that you two left Alice cleaning the store alone, again, so that you could come to this game."

Who are these people? How do they know Alice? What do they have to do with our Company business? The brothers began to leave the arena, while shooting us some very ugly looks.

"Wait a minute!" I yelled. "What are you talking about?"

Brother Tom explained, "Every Sunday you leave that little old woman alone to load the truck with quarters of beef. Those things weigh over ninety kilos! Your superiors will be hearing of this! We should not have to help that woman every Sunday so that you two can be lazy!"

Alice was the last person we would have suspected of pilfering ninety-kilo hindquarters of beef. Gordie and I looked at one another and ran back to the store. We arrived just in time to see the tiny woman fling a hindquarter of beef into a waiting pickup truck, as if it were weightless. She then went back for another one.

"It's always the quiet ones," Gordie said. "Always."

ARCHANGEL

Michael was a rather handy guy to have around once you got past his odd appearance and strange mannerisms. Every northern community had a Michael of its own, someone who wasn't quite like everyone else and, in being different, was usually assumed to be the village idiot or outcast. After years of running Hudson's Bay Company outposts, I had learned to bring out the best in all my employees and to respect everyone's contribution, large or small. Michael, in his own way, always gave me his best when I hired him to do simple odd jobs in Split Lake, Manitoba. He also proved to be one of the most clear-headed, courageous people on hand, a real guardian angel, during a catastrophe that could have destroyed the entire community.

The Cree people of northern Manitoba had a nasty habit of sticking unflattering labels onto anyone who was passing through, making waves, or just being different. Michael was called "M & M," not because he liked the candy that promised to "melt in your mouth, not in your hand," but because he stuttered. As a child, when he was asked his name, he would bathe his neighbours in spittle as he forced out "M-MMM-MM-M-Michael." So the name M & M followed him into adulthood as did the assumption that he was a fool. I wasn't sure if he was a fool or not, but I found myself hoping that he was intellectually deficient enough not to notice the terrible treatment he received at the hands of his own people. I met Michael when I first arrived in Split Lake, and although I knew right away that he was generous, I would never have taken him for a hero.

I had operated some very old outposts for the company, but when I arrived at Split Lake in 1983, it looked like the oldest I had yet encountered. I flew into the community in an old single-engine Otter that looked like a tool box with wings. We circled twice as we descended, the post growing larger and more horrible through my tiny porthole of a window. No one had showed up to greet the new manager; however, some clever soul had left the company vehicle beside the airstrip with the keys in it. The cranky pilot and I loaded the truck until it dropped on its axles and then tossed the remaining freight onto the gravel airstrip for a second trip into the village.

Both my teetering load of groceries and I were smothered in fumes as the ancient Otter coughed and hacked itself back to life and bumped its way down the pitted runway. I turned the key to start the company's old Ford panel truck and laughed to myself as the motor awakened. It sounded very much like the Otter, which was now clawing for altitude, trying to escape the bad weather that was closing in.

After five dusty kilometres of bone-jarring bumps, the old Ford seemed to relax as we pulled onto the reserve. I jumped out to survey the scene. I was looking for the familiar red shingles and whitewashed walls typical of most HBC posts and which I had surveyed from the air. The entire place was deserted; the village had not yet awakened despite the racket the aircraft had made coming and going.

The reserve was a tangle of shacks and outhouses scattered about with little rhyme or reason. I had lived on many reserves; most looked exactly like this one. I finally spotted the red shingles I had seen from the air at the western extremity of the reserve and wove my way through the village, trying to find a smooth route to the store. There wasn't one. When I backed the truck up to the rear of the store and cut the engine, I could swear I heard the old truck laugh at me.

The previous manager had left the keys with the pilot when he had flown out the previous day. I had picked up the bundle of keys from the crusty aviator. If there was one constant at any Hudson's Bay outpost, it was that the manager's keys had to number two hundred or more and be unable to fit into even the largest of pockets. In fact, only four keys were ever really needed: one each for the store, warehouses, staff house, and fuel pumps. If a post were lucky enough to have a vehicle, then a fifth key would be necessary. The other one hundred and ninety-five keys? Who knows? Most of them were older than the managers who carried them.

As I was trying the forty-fifth key in the padlock, a slovenly, shabbily dressed, and filthy young man startled me as he stepped from behind the truck and took the keys from my hand. Without a word, he selected the correct key in one go and popped the lock off the door. "Thanks," I stammered. Silently, the young fellow started to unload the truck with great gusto. I could barely keep up with him as he launched the boxes from the back of the truck and into my arms more than two metres away. I replaced the lock and took the valid key off the chain to save time on the second trip. As my ragged partner leapt into the passenger seat of the truck, I introduced myself both in English and in my best Cree. He ignored me in both languages. Oh well, at least one of my employees had surfaced and on a weekend to boot.

The second load was a lot easier, thanks to the efforts of my silent companion. When we had moved the last of the freight into the store, I sat on the boxes and opened a Pepsi for myself and one for my new friend. (One of the lessons an astute post manager picks up quickly is whether a community is a Coke community or a Pepsi populace. This was especially important in the Arctic as huge quantities of the liquid gold were barged in once a year. One mistake and you would have a sugar-driven riot on your hands.) I walked around the darkened store, much of which was already familiar to me. Split Lake, however, was a jumble of buildings randomly nailed together with little regard for levelling or joining floors.

My able assistant followed closely behind me but offered no comments or observations of his own as I carried out a lively dialogue with myself. I pointed to the candy counter and told him that if he was hungry he could take something in appreciation for being the only man standing in the community on a Sunday morning. Totally misunderstanding my gesture, the silent one began to peruse the inventory, foraging for the most suitable victuals. I was amazed as he selected a canned ham, keyed it open on the spot, and consumed the gelatinous confection as I watched. I must have been standing beside the hungriest man in the world.

Shaking his salty and gooey mitt, I thanked my uncouth buddy and sent him on his way. It was getting dark already; it was February and the days were still pretty short. I headed to the staff house with my duffel bag, regretting that I had not asked my employee to select the appropriate key before parting company.

I was never able to sleep my first night at a new post. I lay awake listening to the sounds of the community. Dogs barking, snowmobile engines, someone cutting wood with a chainsaw, and people laughing and yelling in a dialect I had never heard before. My trainee would be back in the morning and hopefully he would fill me in on the community and we could get productive quickly. It was a long night, filled with a thousand memories and the excitement of discovering new people and new places. As difficult as things could get, I was where I wanted to be and could not imagine doing anything else.

In the morning, I was surprised to see a number of local folks waiting at the door for me. I noticed my friend from the previous day was standing by himself, wearing the same soiled clothes. The staff was welcoming and all shook my hand and introduced themselves in both Cree and English. "What about him?" I asked, gesturing to the silent mystery man who was now kicking at the snow with his holey shoes and staring at the ground. Everyone laughed.

"That's M & M!" someone offered as several of the assemblage pelted him with snowballs. "He's a retard! He doesn't work here!"

Without raising his head, M & M shuffled off with a hail of slushy snow pelting him in the back.

"He tries this every time there is a new manager here. He thinks if he shows up someone will give him a job. He can't even speak properly."

Several things suddenly made a lot more sense. His silence, lack of understanding, and grotesque eating habits appeared to be symptomatic of his circumstances. Later in the day, my trainee, Phil, appeared and confirmed what the staff had told me and added that M & M's real name was Michael. I felt terrible for the young lad, but I was overwhelmed with work and my area manager was coming in a few days. The store was a mess.

The Company was attempting to upgrade the store in Split Lake. The HBC had already spent a fortune installing new refrigeration for the grocery department, only to find the ceilings were so low they trapped the heat from the compressors. Six huge air conditioners were then installed. The units not only cooled the store and doubled our power bill, but they also served as revolving doors for thieves. I had been in the community five days and had experienced five break-ins. The last break-in was easy to solve as the desperados had used a Polaroid camera from the display case to photograph how much fun they were having robbing the place. They left the pictures behind for the RCMP.

My sixth night in the village was to be the most eventful. The area manager was due to arrive the next morning for inspection but despite the numerous robberies and the state of the post itself, I wasn't worried. Even though the place was botched, it wasn't my mess and I couldn't possibly have been expected to solve every problem in Split Lake in five days. For example, head office had been badgering the previous manager to paint the interior of the store for months before he left. He procrastinated and then attempted to paint the whole interior by himself, the day before he was transferred. For some reason, he had painted the entire store battleship grey with shiny porch enamel. Years later, I ran into the manager at a meeting in Winnipeg, where he admitted that he was colour-blind and was unable to differentiate between the cans of paint head office had sent.

But it wasn't only the colour of the place that was odd; the former manager's painting method was also evidently askew. The interior looked as if someone had taped a muskrat to a stick, dipped it in paint, and twirled it like a baton. The HBC was more than three hundred years old, yet never before had such a debacle occurred in one of their trading posts.

At 9:20 PM on that fateful sixth night, an agitated elderly woman yelping in Cree beat on my door until she could no longer be ignored in favour of the hockey game. I thanked her for dropping by and closed the door, almost catching her fingers. A few minutes later one of my employees pounded on the door screaming, "Fire!" Phil and I grabbed two fire extinguishers and sprinted to the store, where a small crowd had already gathered.

Smoke was pouring from several orifices of the architectural marvel that was the trading post. I fumbled for my keys, which I had not yet had time to reduce further in number. As I grabbed the doorknob, the flesh on my hand sizzled and stuck to the metal; the fire must have been right behind the steel door. I yelped and dropped the keys into the snow. Suddenly there was a loud burst of sound, and I looked down at my parka, which was now covered with yellow powder. Phil had fired off his fire extinguisher, overlooking the fact that the blaze was inside the building and not on his employer. We were in trouble. The rear door, behind which lay the origin of the fire, was the only possible entry to the building. Because of the many robberies, the store had been fortified with steel bars and metal cladding. My mind was racing.

The buildings in the community were all of wood construction and were packed in way too close to the store. We had four four-thousand-litre horizontal fuel tanks full of gasoline sitting on wooden cribs just a few feet from the building. Split Lake did not have a fire department. And I was responsible for this mess.

The chief and his council quickly appeared on the scene. The chief had a hand-held radio and was calling for his four tribal cops. He asked me what they could do to help. I pointed out that there was no way to stop the building from going up and that we should evacuate all of the houses on that end of the village. The council argued that we only needed to evacuate the homes next to the store. I did not understand what the chief said next, for it was in Cree, but he was pointing at the fuel tanks adjacent to the store.

The tribal cops arrived on the scene, all four dangling from one snowmobile. "We need to evacuate everyone, *now!*" was the only response I had. The snow around the store had already melted and the grass surrounding the fuel tanks was turning brown and smoldering. All four sides of the store were now burning and the roof had just caught. Suddenly I heard a woman scream and saw a man who must have been one hundred years old, trying to start his chainsaw and cut into the side of the conflagration. He kept pulling on the starter rope despite the hot wind from the updrafting blaze taking his hat right off his head. It took two tribal cops to haul him out of there, both scorching their faces as they cussed at him for being so foolish. Foolish? Perhaps. The elder would later tell me that he had trapped for the company for his entire life and so had his father. The old man wanted to save the Bay; it was important enough to him to risk his life.

The wooden cribs under the tanks were now smoldering and we could hear the stack releases on the tops boiling and belching, trying to release pressure. The six air conditioners were going full out, trying to cool the store and had not stopped despite the blaze. I asked the chief, "Is there any way to cut the power to the store to stop those air conditioners from feeding the fire with air?"

The chief ran for the shack of the power company guy who was oblivious to the disaster and had to be roused from a deep sleep. A truck arrived and out spilled the chief and the power guy. They exchanged words and the sleepy technician struggled to put on his tool belt. He approached the power pole nearest the store and eyeballed it as if he was sizing it up for the big climb. He hesitated and then returned to his truck to retrieve another piece of equipment. Our high-voltage saviour then produced a shotgun from the cab of the truck. With a single blast, he cut the wire leading to the store and without a word got back into his truck and went back to bed as if nothing out of the ordinary had occurred. His solution was not by the book, I am sure, but quite practical.

The chief and his entourage reappeared to assure me that the community had been moved back and that tents had been set up to house the elders and children. We turned to look at the building just as a large explosion blew the roof off and the walls began to teeter in. "Let's get out of here!" the chief yelled to all who remained. As we backed away and got into our trucks, we heard a strange noise.

The band owned a bulldozer and a grader that they used to maintain the road into the village. Out of the darkness rolled the bulldozer with a single occupant. The D-8 awkwardly moved between the store and the fuel tanks. The tribal cops yelled and waved the suicidal machine operator away as we prepared to evacuate the last of us. We were thirty metres away from the blaze and were being badly scorched. Whoever was driving that Cat was less than ten metres away; I didn't know how he could bear the heat. We watched as the man and his machine banked snow overtop of the fuel tanks to keep them cool. Several times the snow steamed off the tanks faster than he could bank them. After what seemed an eternity, he smothered the tanks with snow and retreated through the woods to the south of the store.

We were able to watch the fire diminish as there was no longer any danger of the gas tanks exploding. People began to reappear as morning grew near and the danger passed. Finally the store was level to the ground and the only explosions we heard were from the canned food that sounded like popping corn beneath the ashes.

Peter, my area manager, suddenly arrived ahead of schedule. I had left a message at his hotel in Thompson that the store was ablaze. He had brought the area manager from the neighbouring district with him. He thought we would need help planning the fire sale. He had also borrowed firefighting equipment from the Forestry Department. As it was, there was no fire to put out and nothing to sell. Everything was gone. There was no snow within sixty metres of the post with the exception of the banked snow still covering the fuel tanks. I spotted the keys that I had dropped where the back door used to be. Ever the smartass, I presented the keys to my area manager, who was not amused. The only thing left standing was the flagpole on which the charred governor's flag was still flying. I flew that flag for the remainder of my career with the company.

When the smoke cleared, we opened a temporary store in the band's community centre, thanks to the co-operation of the chief and council. The chief and I did not sleep for days as we tried to straighten everything out. A week or so later, we finally had a chance to sit down and talk about the events of the previous days. It occurred to me to ask about the guardian angel who had courageously put himself in peril to prevent the gas tanks from exploding. Apparently the bulldozer had been found back at the band garage where it was usually parked. Much of the paint had burned off, and all of the hydraulic hoses were burned, damaged, and in need of replacement. The driver, well, that had been a mystery to everyone until just that morning, when Michael had shown up at a friend's house asking to borrow a parka. You see, Michael's parka was so badly burned that it no longer kept him warm.

THE HYDRO BOMB

Urban Canadians seem to have an insatiable hunger for electricity. Growth is good, or so we are told, and hydroelectric power is plentiful and cheap. Everyone wins. Neglected in this equation, however, are Canada's Native peoples, who have watched their ancestral lands and traplines become systematically flooded for several generations as a result of growing demands for hydroelectric power. Reserve lands, "given" to the indigenous peoples of Canada generations ago by Her Majesty, are now underwater. Compensation? The land and the aboriginal people on it are interconnected. How do you compensate someone for a human life or for their ancestral lands that are now submerged?

While fishing with an elder named Solomon in Split Lake,

Manitoba, in 1984, I found myself having shore lunch on a point of land directly opposite the community. There were many stone firepits around us, evidence that at one time there had been a large camp on this location. I asked the elder if, in days gone by, the community had once been located on this site. He laughed and told me this story.

After years of negotiation between Manitoba Hydro and the Split Lake First Nation, a dam was built on the nearby river in the 1960s. The resulting reservoir that had formed upriver flooded much of Solomon's trapline and completely flooded the traplines of many other families. No one in the community or with Hydro had anticipated the destruction that had ensued. Negotiations were reopened between the band, Ontario Hydro, and the Department of Indian Affairs. This time around, the negotiations were abusive, violent, and fuelled by anger because the people of the community had lost so much. Part of the final settlement involved bringing power to the reserve at no cost to the band or any of its members. But the process that brought the power to the people took longer than anyone had imagined as the hydro company ran appeal after appeal through the courts.

In the spring of 1968, all the power poles were installed. Then progress stopped. The following spring, massive rolls of cable were left on the outskirts of town. That fall, large barrel-like transformers were mounted on the poles all over the community. The people of Split Lake were unfamiliar with such construction and grew suspicious of what the power company intended. There was no road into the community at the time, and very few of the residents had ever seen transmission lines and equipment.

Rumours began to circulate. Many of the older people in the community felt the young and inexperienced band council and chief had dangerously angered the white people. Word went around that the band had made so much trouble for the white men that the white men planned to kill all the people in the community. The transformers looked an awful lot like bombs. Within days of the rumour starting, the entire community had relocated to the other side of the lake as a safety precaution.

A puzzled line crew arrived to find a ghost town where Split Lake Reserve used to be. They paused in their task in order to call in company representatives and elders from other communities nearby to convince everyone that it was safe to return home. "There were no hard feelings," a representative of the company explained. "We would never think of bombing your community."

It must have worked because the people of the community moved back into their homes.

"They did eventually drop a bomb on us, though," laughed the old man. "You should have seen my first power bill!"

HOMEBREW

I rather doubt that there are many Canadians out there who are aware of the actual length and breadth of this great land. When naming the oceans that surround us, the third ocean at the top of the world is often overlooked. The Arctic Ocean is our longest maritime boundary and is peppered with islands—some as large as provinces, others as small as beluga whales.

With so much to see out there, I really did not mind getting transferred all over the country in order to further my career with the HBC. Actually, that is not altogether accurate. I had threatened to resign and then made peace with the Honourable Company more times than anyone else in its three-hundred-year history. I had a lot of growing up to do and had a great deal of difficulty accepting criticism when I was working so hard and doing my best. Visits from the HBC area managers and accountants were often demeaning and brutal. Even though I appeared to be fickle, the reluctant personnel department, desperate for manpower, flung me around the north like a mosquito in a maelstrom. My poor personnel record wasn't the only factor in deciding my geographical fate. I was also a member of the "Two Hundred Pound Club." The "Pounders," as we were called, were elite only in the sense that we were considered large enough lads to post to the roughest of Native reserves without getting clobbered by the local tough guys.

I discovered myself seeking the familiar in each of the communities to which I was transferred, even though I may have moved a thousand kilometres. I did not spot any definitive similarities, however, save one: homebrew. Keep in mind that I have lived amongst the Inuit of the west, central, and eastern Arctic. I have also made my home amongst the Ojibway, Cree, Dene, and Chipeweyan Indians of the north. Without exception, every culture had a recipe for brew, specific to their piece of geography. Without exception, the RCMP tried, without success, to put a stop to it.

Most homebrew looked somewhat like beer and was brewed for seven to ten days in a bucket or garbage bag, although, in a pinch, I've seen it consumed after three days. One instantly recognizes the magic elixir by its pungent bouquet, murky pigmentation, and the pudding-like sludge on the bottom of the container in which it thrives. Often the liquid gold was garnished with raisins or raisin-like objects, with or without legs, floating on the effervescent surface.

All homebrew recipes had one common ingredient, yeast. As for the rest of the potion's components, viscous or otherwise, anything goes. The list of desired ingredients in any given community would usually match the list of the most shoplifted items at the post. Sugar and blackstrap molasses made sense to me as they are the usual components of beer, but ketchup? In Pikangikum, Ontario, the folks used ketchup and/or stewed tomatoes as the prime ingredient in their hooch. In Baker Lake, Northwest Territories, the local folks would follow us to the dump on their snowmobiles to intercept the rotting fruits and vegetables we were disposing of. In northern Manitoba, raisins, prunes, and figs were the constituent of choice. The community residents of the eastern Arctic employed a wide variety of jams, honeys, and syrups, including Aunt Jemima's butter-flavoured pancake syrup. Northern Saskatchewan people were partial to brewing potatoes, but I believe that was an economic rather than a flavour issue.

In the community of Kugluktuk, which is located on the Coronation Gulf in the western Arctic, the making of homebrew was considered an art form. Having a good homebrew maker in the family was akin to having a family member win a gold medal in the Olympics, but better because the whole family got to stand on the podium. I had elderly shoppers at the post arguing over homebrew recipes that, I discovered, were passed down from generation to generation with great flourish and reverence. The smaller communities were so coordinated that homebrew batches were timed with precision so that at any given time at least two families had a batch ready to share. Unfortunately, the hooch parties, or "smokers," as they were known, usually ended in trouble for someone. Often the participants ended up lining up at the nursing station with digestive ailments as well.

Most RCMP members in the north, who were Arctic veterans, turned a blind eye to the homebrew makers. The constables often had bigger fish to fry and realized how frustrating it was to get a handle on the homebrew situation. The newer officers, many of whom wouldn't know a ptarmigan from a *koomuk*, would challenge the community. Some polar police dared to match wits with the ingenious, inventive, and determined Inuit, only to be humbled by the experience. I have seen huge, muscular veterans of the southern law brought to the threshold of madness trying to outmanoeuvre the homebrew scallywags.

Officer Dave was new at the RCMP detachment in Kugluktuk; he was a very serious guy who had transferred up from the narcotics squad in Vancouver. He was as tough as nails and was determined that Kugluktuk was going to be the place where he earned his corporal stripes. I believe Dave got off on the wrong foot when he flew in Breathalyzer equipment and started pulling over the Inuit on their snowmobiles. The Inuit's lives depended on their snowmobiles. The machines were required to hunt, fish, and trap. The Arctic environment was so harsh that a drunken

~wmobile would be dead sooner rather than later.
that intimately. Most of us could think of more
for the RCMP's manpower and technology. When
~rned from vacation, he promptly confiscated the
redeployed it to Yellowknife while rebuffing his

~ve, although humiliated, was still determined to
end of homebrewing. On several occasions, I
creetly taking notes at my checkout counter. He
~ppers who were buying yeast so that he could
~cks and watch for signs of the evil brew. At one
~ormal request of my area manager to "license"
~uld only be purchased by legitimate makers of
~er Dave became a source of amusement to the
~one who shopped at the post began to pur-
watch him scribble furiously in his notebook.
~ut everyone.
~rning, I was outside the post helping a trap-
~atik and bring his furs into the post. The trap-
~and nodded toward the sewer truck. Because
~rground plumbing and sewage was not possi-
~bove-ground, heated "utilidors" had met with
~arger communities such as Iqaluit. Interior
~ks seemed to be the way to go in the smaller
~ouse or shack had to be self-contained with
~d a sewer tank roughly equal in size. Each
~ed by truck. In bad weather, you could find
~ter for days. Worse yet was the mess you
~wer truck didn't come by to suck out your

sewer tank before it overflowed.

On this particular day, Officer Dave was tailing the sewer truck. The trapper and I watched for quite awhile. Each time the truck stopped to suck someone's tank, the police truck stopped and rolled down the window, which we found curious. My first instinct when encountering a sucking sewer vehicle was either to flee or to roll up my window.

Later that day, I asked the corporal what his overzealous sidekick was up to. Apparently Dave had discovered that after consuming homebrew, a person's urine contained the active yeast from the brew. When the effluent in question was flushed into a sewer tank, the yeast began to work the entire tank. The resulting odiferous result could be detected by tailing the sewer truck and thus identifying the locations of the contraband homebrew labs. Officer Dave would nail the Inuit with their own pee-pee.

Triumphant, Dave returned to the detachment with a rough sketch of the community with a series of Xs marked on it. His plan was to repeat his olfactory survey each week until he had narrowed his suspects down to the most serious brewsters. Dave was filled with braggadocio as he pointed out that it took only basic high school chemistry to trip up and indict his tricky Inuit quarry. Officer Dave accumulated huge amounts of pee-pee data over the final days of winter. He had designs on a devastating series of pre-dawn raids on the unsuspecting criminals.

In the spring, when the sun returns, the Inuit children tend to shed their winter garments too early. This often results in long lineups at the nursing station with complaints of ear infections, chest colds, and walking pneumonia. That particular spring, the Inuit had consumed about twice the normal amount of penicillin usually dispensed in the village. The head nurse was greatly concerned with what was by all accounts an indication that the general health of the Inuit community was in decline.

I was sitting with the nurse and the corporal, shooting the breeze over a hot chocolate, when Constable Dave returned from a potty patrol. He was both angry and puzzled. Despite an entire morning of sewage sniffing, he had failed to detect a single batch of homebrew. Dave was incredulous. We told the nurse of how the young constable had outsmarted the indigenous population with simple high school chemistry. She paused momentarily and then a look of understanding came across her face. The Inuit were dumping penicillin down their toilets so that it would kill the yeast, stopping their sewer tanks from fermenting. The quietest and most humble of people had thwarted the RCMP's youngest and finest, also with basic high school chemistry.

Arctic communities all have above-ground graveyards because of the permafrost. Coffins are placed on the ground, covered with rocks, and marked with a cross. Identical rows of crosses indicated the epidemics that had marched through the communities and seriously reduced the Inuit numbers. Many babies were buried in wooden butter boxes from the HBC. (Baker Lake, NU, 1980)

While I was in Stanley Mission, I grew a mustache to look a bit older. On this windy day of fishing on Lac Laronge, I lost a pickerel-fishing contest and forfeited my mustache in penalty! Needless to say, my coiffure was also ruined by the end of the trip. (Stanley Mission, SK, 1982)

The "Ogoki Holiday Inn" was the local jail, or "crowbar motel," as it was known. Notice the star on the flag—it was meant to impress the Russian government. The chief at the time had applied to Moscow for foreign aid as he felt the Canadian federal government was neglecting the Martin Falls Reserve. (Ogoki Post, ON, 1979)

GABRIEL

It was 1992, and I had come to a crossroads in my life and in my career with the company. The Hudson's Bay Company had recently acquired a chain of stores in Alaska. A couple of our best executives had crossed over to run the new operation that lay to the west of some imaginary line drawn in the snow. The posts were quite similar to ours but had been badly run for years, losing cash on a consistent basis. However, it seemed reasonable to assume that the three-hundred-year-old HBC formula would work in a similar environment, even under a completely different national jurisdiction.

The executives set about recruiting some of the long-term post managers, a practice that, I am sure, was not generally known about at Hudson's Bay House in Winnipeg. Rumours of huge salaries paid in American dollars and multiple yearly excursions to head office in Seattle circled via the moccasin telegraph. If an offer had been sent my way, I intended to decline with great humility and gratitude. I am an all-Canadian guy and the adventure I was on was a Canadian one. Alaska? No thanks! There were many reasons for me not to go; however, my most decisive reason for not defecting was simple. I was not asked.

A few months down the road, my response to the question that was never posed did not matter anyway. The Hudson's Bay Company had decided to divest itself of all operations that did not involve its core Bay and Zellers department stores. Many old-time Canadian retailers such as Eaton's and Woodward's were foundering badly. Numerous American retail juggernaut stores were poised to cross the border and kick the stuffing out of Canada's elite and aging stores. I am not aware of all of the financial machinations that brought this to pass, but I was in a good position to feel the fallout. The good news was that the HBC would live to fight and flourish once again. The downside was that the northern stores, and in particular the inland stores division, would be cut loose from the mother company.

Staff members were offered shares; the rest were gobbled up by moneyed persons in the guise of national bankers and Canadian Tire executives. After three hundred years of history in the farthest flung reaches of Canada, the Hudson's Bay Company in the north ended up being consumed by Canadian Tire. The last thing the Inuit needed was an alternate form of currency bearing the likeness of yet another Scotsman. Both Governor Simpson and his wife, Frances, must have been spinning in their graves. When news arrived that a deal had been struck and that we were now going to be known as Northern Stores Inc., many of us didn't know how to react.

The fur trade had just collapsed the previous season; the remaining trappers were confused and disoriented. A way of life, which the company had brought to the aboriginal people of Canada, was now extinguished. For so long the reason the company was in the north was for the fur. Now, all that was left was a collection of semi-profitable general stores. The Company's relationship with the people was not always cordial, to be mild about it. The aboriginal folks took it rather personally that an industry that once defined their economies, and to a lesser degree their cultures, had been snatched away from them.

Every Company post manager I met throughout my career claimed to have witnessed the end of "the Trade" or the end of the "Old Ways." In retrospect I now believe I also saw the end of the Honourable Company.

In the meantime, I had a barge to unload. I cursed the sky as snow began falling in earnest. We had a difficult time keeping firm footing as we tried to unload the cargo containers stacked near the store. The barge had been extremely late, and we had been concerned that the Coast Guard icebreakers would not be able to cut a path for it in time. It had happened before. In the old days, it meant life or death for a community. Nowadays if the barge did not make it in, huge Hercules aircraft would bring in the supplies instead. But hauling by aircraft would translate into much more expensive goods and fuel for the people of the communities.

It's difficult enough to do your job at forty below without having to endure a diminutive peanut gallery eyeballing you. Gabriel was always watching. Gabriel was a tiny lad, even by Inuit standards, five years old at most. He was a spectator of life from what I could see of his vertically challenged world. He was both an annoyance and a lovable pest.

I was watching carefully for Gabriel that day. He had been watching my crew unload the containers. He had introduced himself to everyone already and had been knocked off his feet several times. As huge, heavy cases and bales of groceries were passed from man to man, chain gang style, Gabriel had inserted himself into the line several times and had been clobbered by the freight. He would gamely pick himself up and get back into line. At one point one of the men picked him up and passed him down the line into the warehouse, where I was asked to deal with him.

I took Gabriel across the street beside the store and asked him which house was his. There was no one home at any of the three houses he brought me to. He claimed to have forgotten which house was his; they all looked so much alike. Several inches of snow had accumulated, and I was holding the little guy's hand so he would not dart out under the approaching snowplow. Nearing the end of his run, the plow banked a huge heap of snow up against the telephone pole in front of the row of houses that all seemed to belong to the little fibber. I took a shovel and cut a "snow couch" into the top of the heap. I planted Gabriel on the bank and asked him to stay off the road and away from the vehicles. He did.

For the remainder of the time we spent unloading the barge, Gabriel sat on the permanent perch I had made for him on top of that snowbank. From there he could watch the comings and goings of the adult folk and the many vehicles of the community. Gabriel loved vehicles; his favourite was the sewer truck, although he also held the RCMP truck in high regard. I believe he liked them both because people would scatter when they drove by, although for entirely different reasons.

Every morning during that resupply period, on my way to work, Gabriel was up on his perch, waving and wiping his nose with his scruffy mitt. Every morning he had a dirty face and I wondered where this child found dirt in this white Arctic landscape. Every morning he introduced himself as if he had never met me before.

Two memos arrived from head office on a Wednesday three weeks after the barge had departed. The first was an enquiry about why all of the cargo containers had not been returned on the barge. We would now have to rent them at great expense for an entire year until the following resupply. I replied that we were out of warehouse space and were using the containers as temporary "cold" warehouses to shelter the freezable groceries until we could expand the warehouses and the store. The community had outgrown the post years ago; several frustrated managers had come and gone after trying to resolve the dilemma. Their pleas seemed to fall on deaf ears.

One of the old-timers, my first area manager, had shared a three-part parcel of wisdom with me while we polished off a bottle of rye:

1. Keep your reproductive apparatus out of the payroll.
2. You can't make a living window dressing.
3. If you don't have the tools, you can't do the job.

Without warehousing, we did not have the tools to do the job. That area manager was long gone and it appeared common sense had left with him.

The second memo indicated that, although we were now part of Northern Stores Inc., we would be allowed to keep the old HBC signage up for three more years. I suppose that was some consolation; I didn't want to be the guy to hoist a Canadian Tire banner at this Arctic outpost.

Something died in me when the fur trade went under. I had to look into the leathery faces of many elders and watch their hearts break. Some had trapped anyway and brought me their furs, as they could not, they would not, believe that I was telling the truth. I watched their hearts break again as the reality and truth of it made its way to their core. Many of the toughest men I had ever met cried. I cried with them, for there was nothing else to be done. Although there was talk of fur markets and prices bouncing back in a few years, I kept it to myself, as I could not bear to bring hope to the trappers only to take it away from them again.

Before long the trappers were on welfare. Sales dropped through the floor and I did not know if any of us were going to make it. Because most communities had television by that time, it was possible to walk through the community and not see any-one working on their snowmobile or komatik. All was quiet, and the blue glow of television screens illuminated the night through every window.

Gabriel, however, did not seem interested in television. He stayed on his snowbank until dark and then made his way home, dropping his pocket cars, which always overloaded his pockets. I watched him wander away and I wondered what kind of future he would have. I was curious about what kind of future the entire community would have.

I once had a Cree friend with whom I went fishing frequently in Sandy Lake, Ontario. It had been several days since I had helped him unload his mother from a stretcher. She had come home on a medivac, returning to die amongst her family on their ancestral lands. Knowing his mother only had hours to live, he asked me to go fishing with him. I was surprised but agreed to go. I asked him how he could fish when his mother lay dying. He replied to me in Cree, which I did not understand. Later, as we headed home, we stopped by the falls to watch the sun set behind the tamaracks and pines. We smelled the spring air coming alive with budding leaves and new grasses. We heard the birds calling to one another to begin life anew. As he dropped tobacco into the water to thank the lake for the fish and to thank the sun for the exquisite day, he turned to me and said, "I love her too much to watch her die."

That is how I felt as I watched Gabriel go home, dropping his toys in the snow. That is how I felt when I looked into the heartbreaking faces of the elders and trappers. That is what was in my heart as I read the memo about the demise of the Honourable Company. I loved them too much to watch them die. I had a decision to make.

A few days after the memos arrived, we were finally down to one last cargo container. I realize that does not sound like much, but those containers hold nearly seventy-five hundred kilograms of freight each. The metal monsters could accommodate two half-ton trucks parked bumper to bumper. It was slowing things down too much to spend several hours a day reshuffling stock between the warehouses and the containers. Everyone agreed to work overtime to finish the lingering job once and for all. As the crew got busy, I found the time to take a break and have dinner at the local hotel for a change. Two non-indigenous teachers from the community had decided to marry after a full year of secretly canoodling, to the delight of the Inuit. The Inuit would tease white people who did not have sexual partners as they felt it was an unnatural state of affairs. Frequently the Inuit drew on their own numbers to attempt to remedy the situation, often with great success.

After a dinner of caribou stew, bannock, and "traditional" Kraft macaroni and cheese, some hero produced six bottles of the worst plonk I have ever tasted. The principal of the school had secretly squeezed some grapes and come up with an almost indescribable vintage. It assaulted the senses, tweaked the nose, numbed the tongue, and thrashed the throat on the way down. The most notable side effect was that all of our teeth immediately turned black. All the same, it was a happy occasion and the extreme alcohol content of the hooch began to kick in. Someone popped a tape into the eight-track player in the corner and Trooper began to spew from the ancient speakers. I did not know that teachers liked to dance as much as they did that night. It seems a year without any alcohol makes for a room full of cheap drunks dying to let their hair down.

As the evening descended to new lows of debauchery, a couple of my crew burst into the room looking for me. We stepped outside and I warned them that if they had not finished unloading that last container they would have to come back inside and dance with drunken *kabloonaat* educators and all bets were off. They informed me that there had been a shooting in town. Just then we heard several quick bursts of gunfire. Looking about town, we could see that many people had turned off all the lights in their houses.

"Where are the guys?" I asked.

They were all safely inside the cargo container, which had already been struck by a couple of bullets. There was snow everywhere and it muffled what little sound there was in the community.

Wump … wump, two more shots. A woman ran by us, crying. Someone was walking through town with two rifles, reloading and firing randomly through people's windows. *Wump …* another shot. We couldn't tell where the shots were coming from.

"Get back to the container and keep everyone in there!" *Wump, wump, wump.*

"He's near the Bay!" someone yelled, running in the opposite direction. The RCMP truck flew by, a grim-faced, white-knuckled officer behind the wheel. His partner was out of the community escorting a prisoner. He was wearing his body armour, which was something I hadn't seen very often in the north. From the sound of those weapons discharging, they were high-calibre, and I don't believe the body armour would have offered much protection. At least one of the rifles sounded like a semi-automatic as well.

We followed the police truck to a house just in time to see the officer toss a suspect into the back of the truck. We had come to see if we could be of any help as a single officer would not be in a good situation in a gunfight. "Is there anything I can do to help?" I asked the corporal. He turned to me and for the first time ever or since I saw an RCMP officer crying. He was a hulk of a man who had once worked undercover in Vancouver, busting drug dealers and bikers. He was one of the toughest men I had ever met. And he was crying. He got into the truck and headed back to the detachment. A few hours later, an RCMP tactical unit and a couple of detectives arrived in an aircraft. A crowd had now gathered and Samuel, one of the town's finest hunters and leaders, emerged from the house. He walked away silently.

We walked to the cargo container, and the guys were already standing outside in a circle. There was blood on the snowbank at the side of the road. "Was anyone hit?" I asked. Everyone was scared; no one was hurt. "What's with the blood then?" They looked at each other, no one wanting to tell me the news.

"It was Gabriel. A bullet hit the road, bounced up, and hit him in the knee," one of the crew said. Gabriel's uncle Angus had scooped him up and run to the nursing station with him. We all walked together to the nursing station, where a crowd had begun to form. We took our time because none of us wanted to see the little guy hurt. Gabriel's sobbing father slowly opened the door and, supported by a sullen-faced nurse, addressed the crowd in Inuktitut.

Gabriel was dead.

Our little friend had indeed been wounded in the knee. However, when he was undressed for medical attention, the nurses noticed that a .303 round had passed through a wall, bounced on the gravel road, and struck him in the chest. He had almost been cut in half. The .303 British rifle and cartridge were designed during the First World War to fire long distances from trench to trench. They make a hell of a mess, but to this day aboriginal people still use them to knock down moose, caribou, and polar bears. The rifles are inexpensive and are able to withstand the rugged Arctic conditions faced by the Inuit hunter. They are still used to train military Canadian Rangers in the north.

Gabriel had been standing on his snowdrift watching my employees unload the last container. He was blown off the slope, scattering his life's blood and pocket cars in every direction.

The horror of it took my heart and my breath away.

I later found out that Samuel had followed the drunken gunman into a house and had pounced on him when he had stopped to reload after shooting the place up. Samuel was a hero, but he sure did not feel like one. While he waited for his chance to subdue the gunman, several shots had penetrated the walls. Those were the shots that had hit little Gabriel after skipping on the surface of the road. Samuel had been a little late and blamed himself. No one else did.

The funeral had to wait awhile because in the case of wrongful death an autopsy is always ordered, and the body would be sent to Montreal. I tried not to picture the little ragamuffin autopsied, but the image would not stay out of my mind. The community used the time Gabriel was away to mourn and to tear a grave into the permafrost.

On the morning that Gabriel came home, the snow buntings were preparing to leave us for the winter. The Inuit believe that the buntings are so tiny and so delicate that God scoops them up each year and keeps them warm in heaven until the sun returns to the frozen land. He then casts them back down so we may enjoy their beauty. I did not attend the funeral, but I heard that Gabriel was buried with his pocket cars and a new parka. The coffin was carried on the fire truck, which Gabriel would have approved of, I am sure. It was his third favourite vehicle because when it came around, everyone ran towards it.

The sun left us as it always did. It proved to be the longest winter I had ever experienced in the north, and I wished God would scoop me up and keep me with the buntings, warm in heaven until spring. Every day I had to walk to work past that same snowbank. Several times in the permanent twilight I thought I saw the little curmudgeon out of the corner of my eye.

During the winter darkness, I often found more thinking time than I cared to have. But dark days are good thinking days all the same. I thought and waited for the buntings to come back. I, too, wanted to be reborn in some way.

Every good trader knows when it is time to take stock. I decided that winter that I had to take stock of my own life. I had come to the north a child; I was now a man. I had embraced the aboriginal people and they had saved me: they showed me who I was and helped me find my purpose. The Company, good or bad, is what brought me to where I was in my life; it had showed me my strengths. I felt that so much had happened. The Honourable Company was gone from the north. The trappers were lost and living with despair. How were the Inuit people going to survive, and in what kind of world would they have to live?

By spring, I had resolved my quandary. I decided to leave the northern outposts and communities, and to leave the aboriginal peoples who live there. I found in my heart that I loved them too much to watch them die.

ABOUT FIFTH HOUSE

Fifth House Publishers, a Fitzhenry & Whiteside company, is a proudly western-Canadian press. Our publishing specialty is non-fiction as we believe that every community must possess a positive understanding of its worth and place if it is to remain vital and progressive. Fifth House is committed to "bringing the west to the rest" by publishing approximately twenty books a year about the land and people who make this region unique. Our books are selected for their quality, reader interest, saleability, and contribution to the understanding of western-Canadian (and Canadian) history, culture, and environment.

Look for the following Fifth House titles at your local bookstore:

Country Calls: Memories of a Small-town Doctor
by Dr. Sid Cornish with Judith Cornish

Don't Name the Ducks and Other Truths about Life in the Country
by Wendy Dudley

Five Pennies: A Prairie Boy's Story
by Irene Morck

Just Another Indian: A Serial Killer and Canada's Indifference
by Warren Goulding

North to Cree Lake: The Rugged Lives of the Trappers Who Leave Civilization Behind
by A. Karras

The World Is Our Witness: The Historic Journey of the Nisga'a into Canada
by Tom Molloy with Donald Ward